T0316324

Travelling Languages

Based on the commonly held assumption that we now live in a world that is 'on the move', with growing opportunities for both real and virtual travel and the blurring of boundaries between previously defined places, societies and cultures, the theme of this book is firmly grounded in the interdisciplinary field of 'Mobilities'. 'Mobilities' deals with the movement of people, objects, capital, information, ideas and cultures on varying scales, and across a variety of borders, from the local to the national to the global. It includes all forms of travel from forced migration for economic or political reasons, to leisure travel and tourism, to virtual travel via the myriad of electronic channels now available to much of the world's population. Underpinning the choice of theme is a desire to consider the important role of languages and intercultural communication in travel and border crossings; an area which has tended to remain in the background of Mobilities research.

The chapters included in this volume represent unique interdisciplinary understandings of the dual concepts of mobile language and border crossings, from crossings in 'virtual life' and 'real life', to crossings in literature and translation, and finally to crossings in the 'semioscape' of tourist guides and tourism signs.

This book was originally published as a special issue of *Language and Intercultural Communication*.

John O'Regan is Senior Lecturer in Languages in Education at the Institute of Education, University of London, UK. His research interests lie in intercultural communication, cultural studies, critical discourse analysis, globalization and the new capitalism, and the development of English in diverse world contexts.

Jane Wilkinson is Lecturer in German at the University of Leeds, UK. She was Chair of the International Association for Languages and Intercultural Communication (IALIC) between 2008 and 2010. Her research focuses on borders and border crossings in contemporary German-speaking culture, and she is the author of *Performing the Local and the Global: The Theatre Festivals of Lake Constance* (2007) and several articles on cross-border cultural events at the German-Polish border.

Mike Robinson holds the Chair of Cultural Heritage at the University of Birmingham, UK, and is the Director of the Ironbridge International Institute for Cultural Heritage. He has research interests in tourism as a mechanism for intercultural dialogue and tourist cultures.

Travelling Languages

Culture, Communication and Translation in a Mobile World

Edited by
John O'Regan, Jane Wilkinson and Mike Robinson

LONDON AND NEW YORK

First published 2014
by Routledge
2 Park Square, Milton Park, Abingdon, Oxon, OX14 4RN, UK

and by Routledge
711 Third Avenue, New York, NY 10017, USA

Routledge is an imprint of the Taylor & Francis Group, an informa business

© 2014 Taylor & Francis

British Library Cataloguing in Publication Data
A catalogue record for this book is available from the British Library

ISBN 13: 978-0-415-73937-5

Typeset in Times New Roman
by Taylor & Francis Books

Publisher's Note
The publisher accepts responsibility for any inconsistencies that may have arisen during the conversion of this book from journal articles to book chapters, namely the possible inclusion of journal terminology.

Disclaimer
Every effort has been made to contact copyright holders for their permission to reprint material in this book. The publishers would be grateful to hear from any copyright holder who is not here acknowledged and will undertake to rectify any errors or omissions in future editions of this book.

Contents

Citation Information   vii
Notes on Contributors   ix

Introduction: Travelling languages: culture, communication and
translation in a mobile world
John O'Regan, Jane Wilkinson and Mike Robinson   1

1. Crossing borders virtual and real: a transnational Internet-based
   community of Spaghetti Western fans finally meet each other face
   to face on the wild plains of Almeria, Spain
   Lee Broughton   6

2. Crossing the intercultural borders into 3rd space culture(s): implications
   for teacher education in the twenty-first century
   Melinda Dooly   21

3. Figuring home: the role of commodities in the transnational experience
   Christine Penman and Maktoba Omar   40

4. Language and the negotiation of identity and sense of belonging: a study
   of literary representations of Indians in England
   Meenakshi Sharma   53

5. Travelling languages? Land, languaging and translation
   Alison Phipps   66

6. Portuguese 'to go': language representations in tourist guides
   Maria João Cordeiro   79

7. 'Please don't climb trees and pick flowers for the sake of life' – making
   sense of bilingual tourism signs in China
   Oliver Radtke and Xin Yuan   91

Index   109

Citation Information

The chapters in this book were originally published in *Language and Intercultural Communication*, volume 11, issue 4 (November 2011). When citing this material, please use the original page numbering for each article, as follows:

Introduction
Editorial: Travelling languages: culture, communication and translation in a mobile world
John O'Regan, Jane Wilkinson and Mike Robinson
Language and Intercultural Communication, volume 11, issue 4 (November 2011) pp. 299–303

Chapter 1
Crossing borders virtual and real: a transnational Internet-based community of Spaghetti Western fans finally meet each other face to face on the wild plains of Almeria, Spain
Lee Broughton
Language and Intercultural Communication, volume 11, issue 4 (November 2011) pp. 304–318

Chapter 2
Crossing the intercultural borders into 3rd space culture(s): implications for teacher education in the twenty-first century
Melinda Dooly
Language and Intercultural Communication, volume 11, issue 4 (November 2011) pp. 319–337

Chapter 3
Figuring home: the role of commodities in the transnational experience
Christine Penman and Maktoba Omar
Language and Intercultural Communication, volume 11, issue 4 (November 2011) pp. 338–350

Chapter 4
Language and the negotiation of identity and sense of belonging: a study of literary representations of Indians in England
Meenakshi Sharma
Language and Intercultural Communication, volume 11, issue 4 (November 2011) pp. 351–363

Chapter 5

Travelling languages? Land, languaging and translation
Alison Phipps
Language and Intercultural Communication, volume 11, issue 4
(November 2011) pp. 364–376

Chapter 6

Portuguese 'to go': language representations in tourist guides
Maria João Cordeiro
Language and Intercultural Communication, volume 11, issue 4
(November 2011) pp. 377–388

Chapter 7

*'Please don't climb trees and pick flowers for the sake of life'
– making sense of bilingual tourism signs in China*
Oliver Radtke and Xin Yuan
Language and Intercultural Communication, volume 11, issue 4
(November 2011) pp. 389–407

Please direct any queries you may have about the citations to
clsuk.permissions@cengage.com

Notes on Contributors

Lee Broughton is a Leverhulme Trust Early Career Fellow in the Centre for World Cinemas at the University of Leeds, UK. The Frank Parkinson Scholarship funded his doctoral research, which questioned Hollywood's claim to fundamental ownership of the Western genre by critically examining key but previously overlooked European Westerns. His recent publications include 'Upsetting the genre's gender stereotypes: *Ramsbottom Rides Again* (1956) and the British out West' (*International Westerns*, 2014) and '*Captain Swing the Fearless*: a Turkish film adaptation of an Italian Western comic strip' (*Impure Cinema*, 2014).

Maria João Cordeiro studied Modern Languages and Literatures (English and German Studies) in Lisbon, Portugal, Trier and Hamburg, Germany. She received her MA in German Studies from the New University of Lisbon in 1998 with a dissertation on literature and cinema. In 2008, she earned her PhD in German Studies with a project that focused on the tourist representation of Portugal in German guidebooks and travel articles. She is currently Professor at the Beja Polytechnic Institute and a member of the Research Centre for Communication and Culture at the Catholic University of Portugal.

Melinda Dooly is Lecturer at the Education Faculty, Universitat Autònoma de Barcelona, Spain. She teaches Methodology of English as a Foreign Language (TEFL) and research methods courses, focusing on telecollaboration in education at both undergraduate and graduate levels. Her research addresses teacher preparation and the use of technology to promote enhanced language learning.

John O'Regan is Senior Lecturer in Languages in Education at the Institute of Education, University of London, UK. His research interests lie in intercultural communication, cultural studies, critical discourse analysis, globalization and the new capitalism, and the development of English in diverse world contexts.

Maktoba Omar is a Reader in Marketing Strategy and a member of a range of professional organisations. She has published and acted as editor and referee for a number of academic journals and performed as track chair, presenter and member of the Vetting Panel for a number of national and international conferences. She has won the Emerald Literati Network Outstanding Paper Award 2008. She also acted as consultant and leading academic in a number of projects and company roles, and has generated a substantial amount of funds in the UK and overseas.

Christine Penman is Lecturer in French for undergraduates and in Advertising as Cultural Discourse on MSc programmes in the School of Marketing, Tourism & Languages at Edinburgh Napier University, UK.

Alison Phipps is Professor of Languages and Intercultural Studies at the University of Glasgow, UK, where she is Co-Convener of Glasgow Refugee, Asylum and Migration Network (GRAMNET).

Oliver Radtke is a PhD candidate working on the theme of Chinglish, a rather peculiar yet creative mix of the Chinese and English languages. He was awarded an MA in Modern Chinese Studies from Heidelberg University, Germany, and Shanghai International Studies University, China. His thesis dealt with the sociopolitical relevance of the Chinese blogosphere. He has published three books entitled *Welcome To Presence: Abenteuer Alltag in China* (2007), *Chinglish: Found in Translation* (2007) and *Chinglish: Speaking in Tongues* (2009). He is also the founder-moderator of www.chinglish.de, the online museum for all things Chinglish.

Mike Robinson holds the Chair of Cultural Heritage at the University of Birmingham, UK, and is the Director of the Ironbridge International Institute for Cultural Heritage. He has research interests in tourism as a mechanism for intercultural dialogue and tourist cultures.

Meenakshi Sharma received her MA (Research) and PhD from the University of Queensland, Australia. She is currently Associate Professor in Communication at the Indian Institute of Management, Ahmedabad, India. Her research focuses on Management Communication, Post-Colonial Theory and Literatures, and Cultural Studies. Her publications include the books *Postcolonial Indian Writing in English: Between Co-option and Resistance*; *Speak with Impact*; and articles in books and refereed journals.

Jane Wilkinson is Lecturer in German at the University of Leeds, UK. She was Chair of the International Association for Languages and Intercultural Communication (IALIC) between 2008 and 2010. Her research focuses on borders and border crossings in contemporary German-speaking culture, and she is the author of *Performing the Local and the Global: The Theatre Festivals of Lake Constance* (2007) and several articles on cross-border cultural events at the German-Polish border.

Xin Yuan studied Applied Linguistics and specified in Teaching English as Second Language (TESOL), Second Language Acquisition (SLA) and Child Language Acquisition. She studied in the National Research Center of Foreign Language Education in Beijing Foreign Studies University, China, and is now a PhD candidate with the Junior Research Group of 'Transgressing Language and Intercultural Communication Spaces and Identities in Urban Arenas – the Case of Harbin' with the Cluster of Excellence: 'Asia and Europe in a Global Context' at the University of Heidelberg, Germany.

INTRODUCTION

Travelling languages: culture, communication and translation in a mobile world

This issue of *Language and Intercultural Communication* features a selection of the papers presented at the tenth annual conference of the International Association for Languages and Intercultural Communication (IALIC) in association with the Centre for Tourism and Cultural Change at Leeds Metropolitan University in December 2010. The theme of this tenth anniversary conference, chosen to highlight and explore research synergies in the fields of intercultural communication and tourism, was *Travelling Languages: Culture, Communication and Translation in a Mobile World*. Based on the commonly held assumption that we now live in a world that is 'on the move', characterised by growing opportunities for both real and virtual travel and the blurring of boundaries between previously defined places, societies and cultures, the theme is firmly grounded in the interdisciplinary field of 'Mobilities'. 'Mobilities', a term coined and developed by Sociologist John Urry at the turn of the twenty-first century (see, for example, Urry, 1999; 2007), deals with the movement of people, objects, capital, information, ideas and cultures on varying scales, and across a variety of borders, from the local to the national to the global. It includes all forms of travel from forced migration for economic or political reasons, to leisure travel and tourism, to virtual travel via the myriad of electronic channels now available to much of the world's population. Underpinning the choice of theme was a desire to consider the important role of languages and intercultural communication in travel: an area which has, perhaps surprisingly, tended to remain in the background of Mobilities research. When we travel abroad or enter into virtual relationships and transactions with organisations or individuals in other parts of the world, we often encounter new languages and have to develop new means of communication and interaction, whether by learning new languages ourselves or by seeking the assistance of intermediaries. In both cases, some form of translation between languages and cultures is involved and a degree of intercultural competence, a concept much analysed and debated in the pages of this journal, is required. Scholars with an interest in intercultural communication, language education, and linguistic and cultural translation thus have potentially much to contribute to the Mobilities debate, as is clearly demonstrated in the seven contributions to this Special Issue.

The papers which are included in this Special Issue represent eclectic understandings of the dual concepts of mobile language and border crossings, from crossings in 'virtual life' and 'real life', to crossings in literature and translation, and finally to crossings in the 'semioscape' of tourist guides and tourism signs. In the way in which the papers have been arranged in this issue they more or less correspond to one of these dimensions. Thus, the first pair of papers, by Broughton and Dooly respectively, are concerned with border crossings in cyberspace, and with the paper by Penman and Omar form part of a trio which are devoted to borders both virtual and real. In his paper, Lee Broughton explores the culturally productive activities of a transnational virtual community of Spaghetti Western fans, who come together on an Internet message board called the *Spaghetti Western Web Board*. The paper presents a detailed examination of the participatory activities of this select group of film fans. As such it aims to demonstrate that this transnational body of Spaghetti Western fans, who cross virtual borders in order to communicate with each other online, are a 'virtual community'. By using theories connected to virtual communities, new technologies, fan cultures and tourism, Broughton seeks to show how the culturally productive activities of this transnational virtual community of Spaghetti Western fans resulted in some of their number crossing real borders and meeting each other face to face on the suitably dust-blown plains of Almeria in Spain, the object of their individual sojourns being the iconic sets and locations of their shared passion – the Spaghetti Western film genre. In his paper Broughton shows how this internationally disparate group of individuals has evolved into a state of 'virtual togetherness' which inspires them to travel across real borders to meet one another in person. Broughton documents how the virtual space which has motivated the fans to become physically 'visible' to one another also has its melancholy obverse, in that the real spaces where they meet, of iconic film set locations and shoots, are suffering their own decline, and steadily becoming invisible to the people who value them most.

Melinda Dooly's paper complements Broughton's by also being focused on intercultural communication in virtual space. Where the focus of Broughton's paper is more generally sociocultural, Dooly's is pedagogic, and concerns a year-long network-based exchange between two groups of student teachers; one group in Catalunya (Spain) and the other group in Illinois (USA). The student teachers were involved in various collaborative activities during their online exchanges, and Dooly's paper looks principally at the student teachers' collaborative designing of teaching sequences and podcasts. She shows how the participants' online interaction was facilitated through diverse communicative modes such as Skype, Moodle, Voicethread and, interestingly, the online 3D virtual environment of *Second Life* (*SL*), where the participants adopt avatars (virtual representations of themselves) in order to interact with one another while undertaking a series of activities. Dooly's paper is a timely revisitation and augmentation of a discussion which was instigated in a previous issue of this journal by Diehl and Prins (2008), who examined intercultural literacy and cultural identity in *SL*. In her paper Dooly answers the call of Diehl and Prins for research into the educational potential of *SL* for intercultural learning and the development of Intercultural Communicative Competence (ICC). Dooly argues that ICC is a key element for success and/or a possible stumbling block in virtual interaction, and so, following Bhabha (1994) she interrogates what ICC in this type of 'third space' may mean. The evolution of virtual communication by means of *SL* and other online forums such as *Facebook*, which can also involve the anthropomorphic 'degendering' and reincarnation of online interactants, implies the development, according to Dooly, of a 'new communication semiotics' which has consequences for the teaching and learning of ICC. In these circumstances Dooly enquires whether language learning and intercultural education should now incorporate within them a 'critical intercultural semiotic awareness' which is more suited to the new media age.

The third paper in the theme of virtual and/or real border crossings concerns neither humans specifically, nor avatars, nor virtual worlds, but inanimate objects. In their paper, Christine Penman and Maktoba Omar examine the role of material goods in the transnational experience, and people's relationship to these goods when they are in transit between cultures. Of specific interest to Penman and Omar are the kinds of commodities that international students bring from home when living in the UK. Their aim is to provide an emic perspective on cultural flows, in this case of goods as transnational objects. Combining Piercean semiotics with, among others, Bourdieusian and Deleuzean cultural theory, Penman and Omar develop a theme and theoretical construct within which transnational objects appear, and are interrogated, as spatial extensions of the self which connect translocated users, in this case international students studying in the UK, to private conceptions of home. In this circumstance, the authors argue, the goods become part of the students' personal biographies and irreducibly linked to feelings of nostalgia and attachment, and so to the search for 'authenticity' by means of the consumption of objects. The personal investment of individuals in objects as extensions of an imagined self is redolent of Marx's critique of the commodity and of how values of exchange and use come to adhere to it (Marx, 1961 [1887]), and just goes to show that whatever iterations the commodity has gone through, it is still the perceptions of individuals which give it value rather than anything inherent in it. Employing the theoretical frame which they have constructed as an optic, Penman and Omar present, in the second half of their paper, a quantitative analysis of transnational objects such as food, literature, music, toiletries, clothes and fashion, and of the relationship of translocated individuals to them.

Under the second theme in this issue, of crossings in literature and in translation, we have two papers, one by Meenakshi Sharma, and a second by Alison Phipps. In her analysis of literary representations of English-educated Indians in England Sharma examines the experience of language learning and travel, and the myths and illusions which accompany this process. She suggests that under British rule and during the first decades of independence in India, English was taught primarily using literature, and that, as a result, educated Indians travelling to England had clear expectations of the country gleaned from their reading. Moreover, this literary immersion fostered in many Indians a strong sense of identification with an 'imagined' England. Sharma shows how many Indians travelling to England in the 1950s, 1960s and 1970s were surprised to find a country very different to that presented in the literature. She focuses specifically on the depiction of this very specific form of 'culture shock' in fiction and autobiographies before concluding with a discussion of the way in which younger generations of Indians identify with England today. Their exposure to constant multimedia images from the English-speaking world coupled with the growth of English as a global lingua franca creates an even greater sense of confidence and familiarity with the language, people and culture than that inspired by literature in earlier decades. This confidence can, however, still be shattered and expectations disappointed when young Indians travel physically rather than virtually to England.

Physical, bodily experiences are the focus of Alison Phipps' contribution on 'Travelling languages? Land, languaging and translation'. Phipps proposes a new understanding of language and translation as grounded in the land and our relationship with it, and thereby signals a departure from the preferred pairing of language and culture, which sees languages as culturally constructed and mediated and somehow apart from the physical world we live in. She suggests that we inhabit languages in a very similar way to landscapes, i.e. when we learn and use languages, we embody them and experience them physically, a process she calls *languaging*. Building on the concept of languaging, Phipps argues that translation can also be examined as a 'sensory activity' born of our relationship with the world around us which is formed through sight, sound, touch, taste and smell. She uses Brian Friel's play *Translations* and Margaret Elphinstone's novel *A Sparrow's Flight* to analyse the senses and emotions involved in translating and attempting to speak a new language. In both examples the characters find themselves able to communicate their feelings through reference to the land around them and therefore do not share the disorientation of travel presented in Sharma's paper.

Under the third theme in this Special Issue, of crossings in the 'semioscape', we have a first paper by Maria João Cordeiro concerning the language representations employed in Portuguese phrase books and tourist guides, and a second by Oliver Radtke and Xin Yuan on 'Chinglish' in bilingual tourism signs in China. More familiar to many reading this journal will be the term 'linguistic landscape' (cf. Shohamy & Gorter, 2009), for referring to the study of public signage in urban settings, and into which Radtke and Yuan's paper more easily sits. Also, relevant here are the five 'scapes' of Appadurai (1996), ethno-, techno-, finance-, media- and ideo-, to refer to different types of global flow. To this we may add the 'semioscape', to refer to the global flow of signs in the world, and which, in the context of this issue, includes the various 'semio-texts' with which travellers, sojourners and 'border-crossers' in general come into contact, whether in the virtual plane or the real. Into this category the phrase books and tourist guides of Cordeiro's paper readily fit, as do most of the other 'texts' which are documented in the various papers in this issue – as either objects, film sets, online networking sites or as plain written texts. Now is not the time to engage in an extended discussion of the text, or of the semioscape, but it ought to be evident that when we say 'text', we do not confine it to the written mode.

In her paper, Cordeiro, also following Appadurai (1996), employs the term 'languagescape' and addresses what she sees as the lack of research into the linguistic aspects of globalisation. She argues that the success of the ever expanding global travel and tourism industry is largely dependent on removing 'friction' from the interaction between hosts and guests by creating an 'illusion' of a monolingual world through translation, normally into English, of all tourist information, or through the publication of easy-to-use language guides and phrase books for tourists. Using Portuguese guides as a case study, she maintains that these publications at once reassure and motivate the learner by claiming that it will be easy to learn enough of the language 'to get by', but that a little effort will open doors to the 'real' people and culture of the destination. She goes on to demonstrate the way in which such guides 'break' the language, and by extension the culture and people of a destination into easily consumed categories which mask the 'chaos' and complexity of an increasingly fractured multilingual world.

The final paper in this Special Issue 'translocates' the reader to the phenomenon of 'Chinglish', or Chinese–English translations which are to be found on public bilingual signage in the People's Republic of China. After a short review of the existing literature, Radtke and Yuan attempt to establish a typology of Chinglish by means of a corpus-based statistical analysis. The study finds that the majority of so-called 'errors' in Chinglish are due to over-literal translations which are concomitant with a proliferation of grammatical mistakes. In the view of the authors, the disfluency and in some cases nonsensical nature of the Chinglish sign is in large part due to the reliance on machine translation by the local government bodies responsible for public signage. A significant theme in Radtke and Yuan's paper is the decorative use of English in the commercial realm, where the existence of non-Chinese lettering is used to establish, in their view, an appearance of cosmopolitanism by means of English as a given and perpetually iterative 'international brand'. Radtke and Yuan's paper is a salutary reminder of the interminable commodification and reification of English to the point that the presumed language of global communication is so commodified and so reified that its value is reduced to that of a sign which, outside its brandedness, has been emptied of signification.

This Special Issue concludes with two book reviews: Fred Dervin reviews *Introducing Intercultural Communication*, by Shuang Liu, Zala Volčič and Cindy Gallois (Sage, 2011), and Paolo Nino Valdez reviews *The Language and Intercultural Communication Reader*, edited by Zhu Hua (Routledge, 2011).

John O'Regan
Institute of Education, University of London, UK

Jane Wilkinson
University of Leeds, UK

Mike Robinson
Leeds Metropolitan University, UK

References

Appadurai, A. (1996). *Modernity at large: Cultural dimensions of globalization*. Minneapolis: University of Minnesota Press.

Bhabha, H.K. (1994). *Location of culture*. London and New York: Routledge.

Diehl, W., & Prins, E. (2008). Unintended outcomes in second life: Intercultural literacy and cultural identity in a virtual world. *Language and Intercultural Communication, 8*(2), 101–118.

Marx, K. (1961 [1887]). *Capital,* Vol. 1. Moscow: Foreign Language Publishing House.

Shohamy, E., & Gorter, D. (Eds.) (2009). *Linguistic landscape: Expanding the scenery*. London: Routledge.

Urry, J. (1999). *Sociology beyond societies: Mobilities for the twenty-first century*. London: Routledge.

Urry, J. (2007). *Mobilities*. London: Polity.

Crossing borders virtual and real: a transnational Internet-based community of Spaghetti Western fans finally meet each other face to face on the wild plains of Almeria, Spain

Lee Broughton

Centre for World Cinemas, School of Modern Languages and Cultures, University of Leeds, Leeds, UK

Since the rise of the Internet, the act of border crossing has become a pursuit that must necessarily be conceptualized in both real and virtual terms. By using theories connected to virtual communities, new technologies, fan cultures and tourism, this paper seeks to show that the culturally productive activities of a transnational virtual community of Spaghetti Western fans resulted in some of their number crossing real borders and meeting each other face-to-face. My findings are in part supported by evidence collected via a participant observation exercise and e-mail interviews.

Com o avanço da Internet, o ato de se cruzar fronteiras tornou-se um projeto que deve necessariamente ser pensado tanto em tempo real quanto virtual. Recorrendo a teorias sobre comunidades virtuais, novas teconologias, fã-clubes e turismo, este trabalho irá mostrar que as atividades culturalmente produtivas da comunidade de fãs de Spaghetti Westerns, estabelecida num ambiente virtual e transnacional, fizeram com que vários de seus participantes cruzassem fronteiras reais e se encontrassem pessoalmente. Essa constatação é em parte baseada em evidência que obtive por intermédio de um exercício de observação participativa e entrevistas por e-mail.

Introduction

The box office success of Sergio Leone's *A Fistful of Dollars* (1964) resulted in a worldwide vogue for Italian Westerns. Leone's films, and several other so-called Spaghetti Westerns, were released theatrically in America and Britain but hundreds of other genre entries failed to find American or British distributors. American and British reviewers tended to dismiss these films as worthless, ersatz Westerns that lacked cultural roots and the genre eventually came to an end in the late 1970s (see Frayling, 1981). In recent years some Spaghetti Westerns have undergone critical re-evaluations, resulting in new acknowledgement of their cinematic worth. But while Leone's films remain popular, much of the rest of the genre enjoys no public profile. However, cult cinema fans throughout the world do still champion the genre's wider catalogue to this day and a number of these fans now gather together at an Internet message board called the *Spaghetti Western Web Board*.

Having been a fairly regular contributor to the *Spaghetti Western Web Board*, I posted a message on 1 February 2006 explaining my academic interest in fan culture theory and asking whether anybody would object to me gathering evidence and quotes from the board in order to map the fan culture activities that occurred there. I received a number of positive responses and, more importantly, no negative responses. Remaining aware of Seiter's (2000) concerns regarding subjects modifying their behaviour in order to impress their observer, I detected no change of behaviour in any of the web board's members during the course of my ethnographic exercise, which ran for a year. Reference to the identities of the posters quoted, the titles of their messages and the messages' URLs has not been made in order to preserve the posters' anonymity and privacy. Quotes from the message board are simply attributed to the Spaghetti Western Web Board. Those who took part in e-mail interviews were happy to be identified.

This article represents the first detailed examination of the participatory activities of this select group of film fans. As such it seeks in the first instance to prove that this transnational body of Spaghetti Western fans, who cross virtual borders in order to communicate with each other on-line via the *Spaghetti Western Web Board*, are a 'virtual community' (Rheingold, 2000). The test criteria for evidence of virtual community used here is drawn from the work of Denzin (1999), Rheingold (2000) and Bakardjieva (2003). Secondly, this article seeks to map some of the practices of cultural production that are evidenced on the web board. The methodology employed – participant observation and e-mail interviews – is drawn principally from the work of Wakefield (2001) and Bird (2003). Jenkins (1992), Bacon-Smith (1992), Abercrombie and Longhurst (1998) and Hills (2002) have all developed theories connected to fan cultures that are primarily focused upon the activities of fans of cult television texts. I use these theories to test the *Spaghetti Western Web Board*'s members' cultural production, thus proving that fan culture activity can be found amongst cult film fans in this instance.

In the course of doing so, I show that a transnational body of Spaghetti Western fans – who first met each other by crossing virtual borders – were finally moved to meet each other face to face at the Spanish locations where their favourite films were shot. The impetus for this in-person meeting was the circulation of a fan-produced film, Mario Marsili's *C'era una Volta il Western* (2003), whose content suggested that many of the iconic buildings and shooting sites associated with Italian Westerns would soon be lost to the ravages of time or industrial redevelopment. Seen by some participants as a last chance to personally view the remains of the genre's filming locations before they disappeared forever, this in-person group meeting necessarily involved the physical crossing of numerous real world borders. This physical crossing of real world borders in turn resulted in the web board members embarking on a still ongoing mission to capture filmic and photographic records of what remains of Almeria's Spaghetti Western filming locations so that they might be digitally preserved for the enjoyment of future generations. Two films shot during the trip to Almeria and web sites subsequently created by members of the *Spaghetti Western Web Board* were used as the primary research resources for the final third of this article.

Virtual borders, virtual community

Most Internet users' on-line activities reflect their off-line interests too. Hence, fans of *The X-Files* (Wakefield, 2001) and *Dr Quinn, Medicine Woman* (Bird, 2003) are drawn to become members of Internet message boards that are devoted to their favourite television shows. An American citizen, John Nudge advises that he created the *Spaghetti Western Web Board* in 1998 after he realized that some members of a Sergio Leone message board needed a space to discuss Italian Westerns that were not directed by Leone (personal communication, 4 March 2007). While acts of self-disclosure have revealed a transnational membership, with individuals posting from the USA, UK, Canada, Denmark, Germany, France, Japan, Turkey, Australia, South Korea and beyond (Spaghetti Western Web Board – hereafter SWWB – 2006), the board members tend to communicate in English. Anybody with an Internet connection can access the *Spaghetti Western Web Board* and, mindful of the emotional hurt and communal disharmony that the offensive personal attacks known as flaming can provoke, the board carries the following welcome message:

> Hola, Amigo! Welcome to the SPAGHETTI WESTERN WEB BOARD. All posts relating to Spaghetti Westerns are welcome, but, please, no cussing, name-calling or eye-gouging... No slanderous or deliberate attacks on other people will be tolerated... the Marshal and his deputies, have the sole discretion with regard to deleting posts they feel are detrimental to the board... Leave your smoking guns at the Marshal's office or you'll be asked to leave town. (SWWB, 2006)

As if taking its cue from Rheingold's pithy subtitle to *The Virtual Community* (*Homesteading on the Electronic Frontier*) (2000), the welcome message playfully likens the web board to a lawless, Wild West town on the edge of civilization and this sense of play feeds into some posters' messages when they use language associated with Westerns. One member announced their permanent departure with the words, 'adios, amigos y amigas... this board has been a great blessing to me... but... it is time I mounted up and moseyed on down the trail' (SWWB, 2006).

The inherent sense of playfulness found in the use of this kind of Western-themed lingo – known the world over thanks to the popularity and pervasiveness of Hollywood Westerns – plays an important role in the way that some board members communicate and relate to each other. It effectively represents a common vernacular language whose use can play a part in helping individuals from different cultures, who have crossed virtual borders in order to gather together, communicate with each other and feel at ease. As such, the web board remains remarkably flame free and although the board's members are predominantly male, there is little evidence of the kind of confrontational and argumentative 'male styles' of communication that Bird observed in some fan forums (2003, p. 66).

Like many such fan forums, the web board represents an asynchronous form of communication. This means that whenever a message is posted to the *Spaghetti Western Web Board*, other board members are at liberty to post a response in the form of a reply message within their own time, be it hours, days or weeks later. Kollock and Smith refer to these kinds of message boards as '"pull" media' because their core content attracts interested participants who then have to consciously choose which messages they read (1999, p. 6). Messages on the

Spaghetti Western Web Board usually receive multiple replies, leading to an ongoing state of group-based discursive activity, but the resultant message threads have a finite life: stacked in date order, they are automatically deleted after approximately two months.

Jordan indicates that virtual communities literally coalesce around the 'text [being] fired back and forth' by participants on Internet message boards (1999, p. 57) while Denzin asserts that individuals 'establish their presence...[in such virtual communities]...through their regular participation in the conversational topics of the group' (1999, p. 114). Repeated participation on a message board results in the individual establishing a virtual 'personality, self and reputation' (Denzin, 1999, p. 114). In December 2006 a tradition of posting Christmas greetings revealed 48 regular *Spaghetti Western Web Board* posters who might collectively be considered a virtual community (SWWB, 2006). Rheingold describes virtual communities as:

> social aggregations that emerge from the Net when enough people carry on...public discussions long enough, with sufficient human feeling, to form webs of personal relationships in cyberspace. (2000, p. xx)

Nudge observes that 'many of the [*Spaghetti Western Web Board*] regulars joined early [on],...within the first year or so...[and]...we've become good friends over the years' (personal communication, 4 March 2007). Exercises in self-disclosure have encouraged posters to reveal their birthdays, allowing one archivist member to initiate regular 'birthday greetings' messages (SWWB, 2006). Fernback maintains that 'if communication is the core of community, then [a] community is real whether it exists within the same physical locality or half a world away via...telephone wires (1999, p. 213). The *Spaghetti Western Web Board* is a site of much communication, averaging over one thousand postings per month (SWWB, 2006; SWWB, 2007).

Furthermore, actors and directors associated with the Italian Western genre have at times visited the board, sometimes offering first hand testimonies that allow members to add further detail to their personal histories and knowledge of the genre. Nudge observes:

> We've had a number of Spaghetti Western insiders post – Hunt Powers, Robert Woods, Sergio Donati, Aldo Sanbrell, Robert Mark, just to name a few. Dan Van Husen is a regular. One member has struck up a friendship with Nicoletta Machiavelli...[while]...another tracked down Charles Southwood, who everyone thought was just a pseudonym for an Italian actor (he's American, and that's his real name). For years we've been trying to find the name of the man who played Guy Calloway in *For a Few Dollars More*. Last year, out of the blue, his son visited to tell us his father is a Spanish stuntman...[called]...Luis Rodriguez. (personal communication, 4 March 2007)

Most of the professionals that Nudge refers to had their identities confirmed when they were subsequently interviewed for the fanzine *Westerns All'Italiana*.

In seeking evidence that confirms that an on-line gathering is a virtual community, Rheingold adopts and expands upon a schema developed by graduate student Mark Smith (1992), which asserts that 'three kinds of collective goods...[act]...as the social glue that binds' genuine on-line communities together: 'social network capital, knowledge capital, and communion' (2000, p. xxviii). 'Social network capital' is evidenced when ready-made 'real world' communities are accessed via introductions initiated on an Internet message board (Rheingold, 2000, p. xxviii). A real world community of Spaghetti Western fans exists in California and Nudge reports that he and others have accessed this community thanks to 'another board member, [who] has generously sponsored a number of us [non-Californians] to attend the *Golden Boot Awards* in Beverly Hills the last few years' (personal communication, 4 March 2007). Similarly, a New York-based community of Spaghetti Western fans issued the following invite when the soundtrack composer Ennio Morricone performed in the city: 'We are having a pre-Ennio dinner at Virgil's, Saturday at 4 PM, if anyone else is interested' (SWWB, 2007). In both cases, 'social network capital' (Rheingold, 2000, p. xxviii) resulted in a number of American Spaghetti Western fans, that had first come to know each other on-line, briefly meeting in-person for largely social (albeit still genre-related) purposes. By contrast, the sense of transnational participation and cultural production found in the board members' gathering in Almeria, Spain makes that particular real world meeting more significant to my mind and it will be duly covered in detail in section two.

'Knowledge capital' is evidenced when individuals are able to draw upon the collective expertise of an on-line community (Rheingold, 2000, p. xxviii). Nudge notes that some *Spaghetti Western Web Board* members are 'known authorities on the genre ... [who are] ... very generous in answering questions' posted by newer members (personal communication, 4 March 2007). One new poster observed 'through reading the numerous posts on this site [I] find out more info and without doubt learn a lot' (SWWB, 2007). Baym notes that '[together] a large group of fans can ... accumulate, retain, and continually recirculate unprecedented amounts of relevant information' (1998, p. 118). Citing the work of Pierre Levy (1997), Jenkins refers to on-line fandom groups as 'knowledge communities' that possess a 'collective intelligence' (2002, p. 134). Both of these observations would seem to apply to the transnational body of fans that gather at the *Spaghetti Western Web Board*. 'Communion' involves board members offering words of support to fellow members in times of upset or crisis (Rheingold, 2000, p. xxviii) and messages of condolence, support and concern have been expressed on the *Spaghetti Western Web Board*. When a board member auctioned off memorabilia due to unemployment, fellow members posted positive messages: 'you always bounce back ... you'll have a new job soon'; 'hope you find another one real soon' (SWWB, 2007).

Fan cultures and real border crossings

Bakardjieva indicates that a sense of virtual community can lead to a state of 'virtual togetherness' that comes about when 'engaging in different forms of collective practice [prompts] online users [to] transcend the sphere of narrowly private interest and experience' (2003, p. 291). Bakardjieva further argues that 'in all forms of virtual togetherness ... users produce something of value to others – content, space, relationship and/or culture' (2003, p. 294). The *Spaghetti Western Web Board*'s members transfer knowledge and materials over borders both virtual and real in order to engage in culturally productive work that is valued by fellow board members. Much of this work falls within the area of fan cultures. Academics have tended to place fans in one of two positions: discerning active readers who are capable of drawing their own meanings from their chosen texts and creating their own productive fan-based cultures and communities or peculiarly obsessive types who passively consume fantasies created by the culture industry.

Jenkins (1992) has suggested that de Certeau's essay 'Reading as Poaching' (1984, pp. 165–176) can be adapted to give an account of fans that positions them as assertive, discerning and creative. Jenkins observes that de Certeau's '"poaching" analogy characterizes the relationship between readers and writers as an ongoing struggle for possession of the text and for control over its meanings' (1992, p. 24). De Certeau's central argument that reading and meaning-making is an autonomous activity where the reader 'invents in texts something different' to what the authors intended ultimately culminates in a call for a revolution that will overthrow the hierarchical structures that govern reading and consumption (1984, p. 169). Some theorists believe that cult media fans have already enjoyed such a revolution (see Bacon-Smith, 1992; Tulloch & Jenkins, 1995). Brooker and Jermyn assert that, once they have appropriated their source materials, discerning and materially productive fans are able to exist within a 'contemporary form of 'folk' culture' that can be self-sufficient (2003, p. 168). The remainder of this section will examine the materially productive activities engaged in by the *Spaghetti Western Web Board*'s members, paying attention to the effects of new technology on those activities.

Showing scant regard for copyright laws, cult media fans take elements from cult media texts and refashion them within permanent artefacts of their own making (Jenkins, 1992) and fan fiction is perhaps the most obvious example of the poaching process. Observing that *Star Trek* fan fiction writers are mostly female, Bacon-Smith notes that these fans

> are engaged in an act of rebellion. They have stolen characters, settings, plots off the home and movie screens, fleshed them out, created new characters for them to love and given the characters permission to love each other. And all of it is against the law. The characters and settings belong to their creators in Hollywood, who by right of law may demand payment for their use. (1992, p. 4)

Interestingly, the two *Spaghetti Western Web Board* members who produce Italian Western-themed fan fiction – Kim August and Derringdo – are both female. When describing *Star Trek*-inspired fan fiction, Bacon-Smith notes that 'Mary Sue' stories feature young heroines who join the Enterprise's crew for an adventure before dying heroically (1992, p. 53) while 'slash' stories feature homoerotic scenarios where Kirk and Spock form a sexual relationship (1992, p. 229). These two formats have subsequently been used as blueprints by fans of other cult media texts (Bacon-Smith, 1992). However, August and Derringdo's Spaghetti Western-inspired stories are 'character-driven fan fic...[with]...no Mary Sue or Slash [elements]' (August, 2006a).

While Italian Western-themed fan fiction might be uncommon due to a lack of female genre fans, Derringdo (2006) suggests that the genre's directors' habit of occasionally pairing iconic genre characters together means that the crossover fantasies that tend to fuel fan fiction have often already been realized. An obvious example would be *Django Challenges Sartana* (Pasquale Squitieri, 1970), which is one of a number of films that bring two of the Italian Western genre's most iconic characters together. And while many *Star Trek* fans have seen every *Star Trek* episode or film that exists and are aware of their finite number, few Spaghetti Western fans have seen anything like all of the (approximately 460) Italian Westerns ever produced. The knowledge that as yet unseen Italian Westerns still await discovery might reduce the need to produce new genre-related narratives via fan fiction.

For many years the transnational trading of videotapes remained problematic for Spaghetti Western fans because differences in the standards used worldwide for colour television broadcasting meant that tapes swapped between Americans and Europeans had to be converted at some expense from NTSC to PAL and vice-versa. This problem has been eradicated by new technology in the form of multi-region DVD players that will play DVDs from any country in the world. As such, providing access to previously unseen titles preoccupies several of the *Spaghetti Western Web Board*'s members. Their efforts are spread evenly across what Abercrombie and Longhurst term the fans' 'skills continuum', which features the categories cultist, enthusiast and petty producer (1998, p. 144).

'Cultists' are non-professional fans that produce and 'circulate specialized materials' amongst fellow fans (Abercrombie & Longhurst, 1998, p. 139). *Spaghetti Western Web Board* member Franco Cleef is a cultist who poaches liberally from audio and video sources before using new digital technologies and computer software to create English language DVD-R presentations of rare genre titles. His restoration of *The Big Gundown* (Sergio Sollima, 1966) in 2003 is of particular interest. While the most common English language version of the film is 84 minutes long, the full length Italian version runs to 105 minutes. Having made a digital copy of the full length Italian version of the film, Cleef set about finding different broadcast and home video versions of the film that contained English language audio tracks. Cleef reports that an appeal to the *Spaghetti Western Web Board*'s international community resulted in him receiving 'over twenty different versions of the film on VHSs, Betas, U-Matics and dvd-rs, all from different fans who loved the movie and were willing to help' (personal communication, 27 February 2007).

Close comparison tests of all of the different versions allowed Cleef to construct a new and much longer English language audio track that he digitally fused with the Italian video track. Cleef constructed English subtitles for three minutes of the film that still lacked an English audio track. Thirty-seven years after its initial release, English speaking genre fans were finally able to enjoy the full-length version of the film. Making his own DVD-R copies of his restorations and designing his own sleeve artwork allows Cleef to circulate his work to fellow fans at very little cost. His work has inspired a number of other *Spaghetti Western Web Board* members to produce and circulate their own English language restorations on DVD-R.

Ally Lamaj and Eric Mache, two board members who issue Italian Westerns on DVD as a company called Wild East, are examples of 'enthusiasts': those who manufacture niche or specialist items for other enthusiasts, usually within a 'knowable community' (Abercrombie & Longhurst, 1998, p. 148). Wild East is a small company and is unlikely to provide either Lamaj or Mache's main source of income. But their DVDs are professionally manufactured and are stocked by Amazon as well as being sold via Wild East's own web site. Perhaps reflecting the small-scale nature of Wild East's operation, their releases are limited to 1000 units. The company enjoys a special relationship with members of the *Spaghetti Western Web Board* and their releases prompt much in the way of discursive activity on the board. The announcement of each new release prompts the sense of excitement, 'anticipation and speculation' that Hills (2002, p. 176) associates with fans of weekly cult television series. Their release of *Matalo* (Cesare Canevari, 1970) prompted a flurry of posts along the lines of 'has *Matalo* shipped yet?...can't wait to get it-I've heard so much about it!' (SWWB, 2006).

Spaghetti Western Web Board member Ulrich Bruckner is what Abercrombie and Longhurst term a 'petty producer' (1998, p. 148): his work at Koch Media in Germany involves the production of DVDs for the general public at large. Bruckner is the driving force behind the company's Italian Western releases and he admits that 'sometimes it is very hard to convince the president of the company to greenlight' the expensive bonus features (documentaries, interviews, commentary tracks) that he conceives (quoted in August, 2006b, p. 37). The first person testimonies that Bruckner captures in his interviews represent historical documentation to genre fans and Bruckner ensures that English subtitles are placed on any Koch Media Spaghetti Western release that does not feature an English audio track 'as a courtesy to the international fanbase', thus opening up the company's genre releases to English speaking fans world-wide (quoted in August, 2006b, p. 37). One *Spaghetti Western Web Board* member noted 'when I got on this board in june [sic] 2001, there were no Spaghetti Westerns on DVD and I only owned 40 Spaghetti Westerns' (SWWB, 2006). Between them, Franco Cleef, Wild East and Ulrich Bruckner have released close to one hundred Italian Westerns on DVD/DVD-R.

The *Spaghetti Western Web Board*'s 'Marshal', Tom Betts, is the editor of the fanzine *Westerns All'Italiana*. Founded in 1984, the fanzine allowed genre fans worldwide to develop a sense of imagined community in pre-Internet times. An ongoing collection of fan-sourced interviews, articles and reviews, as well as reprints of archival press articles, *Westerns All'Italiana* represents an unofficial history of the Italian Western genre. *Westerns All'Italiana* has recruited new writers via the *Spaghetti Western Web Board* and, in keeping with Jenkins's observation that 'fans have increasingly turned to the Web to lower the costs of production and to expand their reading public' (2002, p. 143), the fanzine has become a Net-zine that is distributed in pdf format free of charge via e-mail.

Digital video cameras and computer editing software have allowed *Spaghetti Western Web Board* members to create their own genre-inspired films. Raymond Isenberg filmed *Once Upon a Time in the Autumn* (2006a), a production that poached soundtrack music and choice clips from genre films. Clever editing – which effectively brought together film footage shot in Spain and Italy during the 1960s and seamlessly merged it with video footage shot in America in the new millennium – allowed the film's lead character (Isenberg himself) to interact with genre characters played by Clint Eastwood and Lee Van Cleef. Isenberg distributed the film on DVD-R to board members with the words: 'the package, disc, and the movie contained therein is provided free of charge to you, my wonderful family and friends...it is a tribute and a gift' (2006b). Isenberg's gifting of his creation to fellow fans is perhaps evidence that supports Burnett and Marshall's assertion that 'despite its recent commercialization,...[a]...gift economy remains at the heart of the web experience' (2003, p. 195).

Mario Marsili's *C'era una Volta il Western* was another fan project that was distributed free to *Spaghetti Western Web Board* members. Shot in the Almeria region of Spain, Marsili's (2003) film was a postmodern hybrid that mixed travelogue and documentary footage with fan fantasy sequences. Hills makes mention of 'cult geographies' and these areas are 'diegetic and pro-filmic spaces . . . which . . . fans take as the basis for material, touristic practices' (2002, p. 144). Parts of Almeria are regarded as 'cult geographies' by Spaghetti Western fans but Spaghetti Western fans do not indulge in the practices of mass tourism. Urry describes how the 'mass tourist travels in guided groups and finds pleasure in inauthentic and contrived attractions' (2002, p. 7). The accounts of fans who search for Spaghetti Western filming locations involve lone travellers who, having been disappointed by the inauthentic nature of commercialized Spaghetti Western tourist sites, depart far from the beaten tourist track (see Billiottet & Perez, 1994; Eustace, 1995; Hodgkiss, 1997). In this sense Spaghetti Western fans are perhaps more representative of what Urry calls 'new tourism', which is 'segmented, flexible and customized' (2002, p. 15).

Hills indicates that when *X-Files* fans track down that show's filming locations, they are replicating 'the narrative structure of the programme' (2002, p. 148). The same might be said of the location-hunting Spaghetti Western fans since many Italian Western narratives involve a search for something: gold, revenge, bounties, etc. Hills observes that 'scouting for *X-Files* locations remains an 'underground' activity in the sense that one cannot simply join a guided tour' (2002, p. 147). The same can be said of scouting for obscure Spaghetti Western locations but a small outfit called Tuco Tours does now offer a package tour of Sergio Leone-related sites (Tuco Tours, 2006).

Before the appearance of Marsili's (2003) film, Spaghetti Western fans tended to visit well-known Italian Western town sets like Mini Hollywood in Almeria but the fans' possession of subcultural capital often spoiled their experience of these commercialized sites. Kevin Grant was irked that the Mini Hollywood set was marketed to tourists as 'pseudo-Americana' as opposed to '*Western All'Italiana*' (1997, p. 4). Recalling an Almerian tour operator's offer of a visit to the towns where *A Fistful of Dollars* and *The Magnificent Seven* (John Sturges, 1960) were filmed, Mike Eustace ironically quips 'a side-trip to Madrid [*Fistful*] and Mexico [*Seven*], eh?' (1995, p. 31). Julian Braithwaite (2003) complains that the Spaghetti Western music tracks played at Mini Hollywood are poor cover versions and, when a re-enactment show's final duel lasts less than twenty seconds, he's outraged: to replicate the genre's conventions the gunmen should have 'stare[d] at each other for 5 minutes at least' before drawing. Urry indicates that individuals seek to '"gaze upon" . . . ideal representations' of views that they have previously internalized via media texts (2002, p. 78). This presumably explains the disappointed fan observations about the commercialized tourist site Western Leone, which utilizes what remains of the McBain Ranch from Sergio Leone's *Once Upon a Time in the West* (1968): '[they should] knock down the added buildings at Western Leone'; '[the] original roof and chimneys [have been] removed and replaced with horrible metallic looking material' (SWWB, 2006).

However, Marsili's (2003) film generated a new impetus amongst the members of the *Spaghetti Western Web Board*: expertly employing the language of film, shots of crumbling adobe buildings juxtaposed with shots of new building developments suggested that some of the hitherto obscure or untraceable filming sites that he had located were in danger of being lost forever. This echoed Gianfranco Pannone's visit to an Italian Spaghetti Western location in the documentary *L'America a Roma* (Pannone, 1998) where he 'soaked up the ambience . . . [because] . . . soon this place too would disappear' and the narrative of the fictional *800 Bullets* (Alex de la Iglesia, 2002), which showed big business effortlessly crushing Almeria's tiny Italian

Western-related tourist industry. Marsili's (2003) film mediated the experience of a trip to Almeria so vividly that several board members from the USA, the UK, France, Denmark, Germany, Spain, Turkey, Japan and South Korea accepted an invitation to meet him there in March 2004, thus crossing real world borders. One attendee, Julian Braithwaite, recalled that

> approximately twenty Spaghetti Western fans descended on Almeria for a week long gathering...arranged through John Nudge's Spaghetti Western Web Board....Many of us have chatted for a long time on the Spaghetti Western Web Board but never before met face to face – but it was like catching up with old friends. (2004)

The Almeria gathering would seem to confirm that 'online ties can be reinforced and broadened through in-person meetings' (Wellman & Gulia, 1999, p. 183).

The trip itself involved two activities: searches for as yet undiscovered Spaghetti Western filming locations and visits to previously found Spaghetti Western filming locations. Throughout the trip the board members appeared as actors in Marsili's latest film, *Per un Pugno di Sogni* (2004). The film's production process was captured in a candid documentary, *The Making of Per un Pugno di Sogni* (2005), which was directed by Cenk Kiral. An early scene in Kiral's (2005) film shows the *Spaghetti Western Web Board* members meeting up at a Spanish restaurant and introducing themselves in English and English is the language that the transnational group uses to communicate with each other for the remainder of the film. Urry notes that tourism sometimes prompts 'playful 'non-serious' behaviour and...relatively unconstrained 'communitas' or social togetherness' (2002, p. 11) and examples of this can be found in both films. Furthermore, when they are seen in their mock Italian Western costumes, the web board members evoke a sense of carnival, which as Bakhtin observed, 'marked the suspension of all hierarchical rank' (1984, p. 10). It is thus possible that the board members' costume-play further acted to put the multicultural gathering of strangers at ease with one another.

Gregory observes that the members of *Six of One*, the appreciation society of the cult British television series *The Prisoner*, regularly visit the show's iconic filming location at the Portmeirion Hotel Village in North Wales and stage costumed re-enactments of key scenes from the series (1997, p. 194). The location remains instantly recognizable and Gregory asserts that fans of *The Prisoner* 'can truly feel they are in "the Village"' (1997, p. 193) – the sinister prison that Number 6 (Patrick McGoohan) repeatedly tried to escape from – whenever they visit Portmeirion. This is not the case with Spaghetti Western fans who, upon arriving in Almeria, are largely confronted by two extremes: disappointingly inauthentic Italian Western-themed tourist attractions or iconic buildings that have become dilapidated beyond repair and familiar vistas that are fast becoming unrecognizable due to new building developments or other changes to the landscape. Rather than making these fans feel that they are in a Spaghetti Western, the eroded buildings and changed landscapes force them to confront the fact that the locations – as they know and remember them from favoured films – will soon be lost forever. Referring to the *Cortijo del Fraile* – the magnificent monastery seen in Sergio Leone's *The Good, the Bad and the Ugly* (1966) – one web board member lamented: 'the rapid deterioration of the mission between 2003 and my return visit in 2005 was painstakingly evident...I fear within 5 years it will just be a pile of rubble' (SWWB, 2006).

Gregory indicates that it is the re-enactment of scenes from *The Prisoner* that has given *Six of One* 'much of its reputation for eccentricity' (1997, p. 194) and Hills (2002) notes that a number of cultural critics assume that some cult media fans are lost in a fantasy world when they relate strongly to favoured media texts and their stars. Interestingly, Bob Spiers' short film *A Fistful of Travellers' Cheques* (1984) actually details the misadventures of two Spaghetti Western fans (Rik Mayall and Peter Richardson) who become lost in their gunfighter fantasies whilst visiting Almeria. However, the members of the *Spaghetti Western Web Board* talk about Almeria in terms of directors and actors and thus reality; '[I] slowly crossed the ... floor to the exact spot where [the actress] Marianna Hill stood some 35 years earlier' (SWWB, 2006); 'to walk where Sergio [Leone], Clint [Eastwood], Lee [Van Cleef], [and] Eli [Wallach] did ... was unbelievable' (Betts, 2003, p. 2). While Marsili's film does feature costumed re-enactments and fan fantasy interludes that employ footage poached from Italian Westerns, Kiral's *The Making of Per un Pugno di Sogni* ultimately serves to reveal the behind the scenes reality of Marsili's filmic endeavours and the trip itself.

Interviewed in Kiral's (2005) documentary, Marsili indicates that the trip to Almeria was a mutually beneficial exercise for both himself and the *Spaghetti Western Web Board* members: Marsili got the actors that he needed to fulfil a lifelong dream of shooting Italian Western-inspired footage in Almeria and the web board members got to visit several iconic filming locations that they would have had difficulty finding without Marsili's expert guidance. A key sequence in Kiral's (2005) film reveals how hard it is to physically locate even the most well documented filming sites. The web board members stayed in a hotel in *Los Albaricoques*, a small village where Sergio Leone shot parts of *For a Few Dollars More* (1965). As the web board members gather outside of their hotel early one morning, the animated conversation that unfolds indicates that some of them have already tried and failed to find the filming location of a memorable scene from Leone's (1965) film. Marsili duly reveals that the scene in question – in which No Name (Clint Eastwood) and Colonel Mortimer (Lee Van Cleef) shoot apples from a tree in order to intimidate a trio of approaching gunmen – was actually shot just a short distance away from the hotel.

Interestingly, the *quid pro quo* nature of the arrangement that brought Marsili and the web board members together proved to be more than just an exchange of mutually beneficial services. In an affecting scene from Marsili's (2004) film, poached footage and clever editing and dubbing allow the director to have a conversation with one of Lee Van Cleef's genre characters. Marsili asks him, 'What's it all about, Spaghetti Western?' He replies, 'It's all about friendship.' Postings on the *Spaghetti Western Web Board* (SWWB, 2006–2007) and subsequent group trips to Almeria and elsewhere serve to indicate that real friendships were forged during the initial trip to Spain in 2004.

Furthermore, the making of Marsili's (2004) film also served to create a kind of psychic link between the web board members and the Italian Western director Sergio Sollima. The film opens with a video message that Sollima recorded especially for the trip's participants: addressing the camera directly, Sollima states, 'Dear friends, I will not be with you physically in Almeria but I'm with you with my spirit and all my heart' (Marsili, 2004). Sollima may not have been there physically but the content of the Westerns that he shot in Almeria during the 1960s actually influenced the various activities that Marsili and the web board members pursued during their stay in the same region over thirty years later. In Sollima's *Run, Man, Run* (1968) the Mexican petty thief Cuchillo (Tomas Milian) is tortured whilst being tied to a sail on a working windmill. In a moving scene from Marsili's (2004) film, web board member Allison McInnes visits what remains of the same windmill and enjoys a quiet moment of contemplation beneath its crumbling walls.

With the palms of her hands pressed flatly together and her outstretched fingers raised to her lips as if in prayer, a close-up of McInnes reveals that she is deep in thought as she takes in the panoramic view that the windmill's location offers. An expertly employed optical effect then results in a close-up of Sollima's face momentarily sharing the shot with McInnes. The director's hands are positioned in the same reverent pose as McInnes' and he too is seen to be deep in introspective thought. Underscored by some appropriately emotional music composed by Ennio Morricone, this shot implies that Almeria's dilapidated buildings can act as symbols that create psychic links that can traverse time and space in order to connect together an imagined community of Spaghetti Western enthusiasts. The sequence ends with McInnes chalking the words 'Grazie [thank you] Sergio' on the side of the ruined windmill.

Later in Marsili's (2004) film, the *Spaghetti Western Web Board* members travel to a location that Sollima used for *The Big Gundown* and they stage a costumed re-enactment of a key scene from that film. As well as shooting his film and guiding the web board members, Marsili also found time to search out previously uncharted Spaghetti Western filming locations. An extra feature on the DVD-R of *Per un Pugno di Sogni* offers some insight into how Marsili and his fellow location hunters go about their business. With his video camera approximating his point of view as he drives along a Spanish motorway, Marsili begins talking the viewer through his mission to find the location of the final duel scene and the monastery buildings that appear in *The Big Gundown*. While watching the film, Marsili (2004) had noticed 'a place with two geological strata: sand and limestone at the bottom and volcanic rock on the top' and he duly drives down a bumpy and treacherously steep dirt track in order to access a mountainous region that he knows has a similar geological make-up.

It has been 'windy, raining and cold all day long' and when Marsili (2004) starts moving about on foot he observes that, 'It is so muddy that I can scarcely walk'. The location hunter soon finds himself walking around a cluster of adobe buildings that he recognizes as the buildings that were used as the monastery in Sollima's (1966) film. The presence of parked cars indicates that the buildings are still in use but the only evidence of life is the sound of an angry dog barking. Marsili (2004) holds a film still up to the camera and observes, 'This is a still of Lee Van Cleef at the duel location and from here, from the "monastery", I have the same view'. When Marsili slowly lowers the still, it is clear that the profile of the landscape that was seen behind Van Cleef during *The Big Gundown*'s final duel matches the profile of the landscape that is now directly in front of Marsili: the presence of a distinctive peak on the ridge of a cliff and a huge but uniquely shaped boulder confirms that Marsili has discovered a hitherto undocumented Spaghetti Western shooting location that can be duly added to the itinerary of the board members' next trip to Almeria.

Hills indicates that when cult media fans produce photographic evidence of a filming location, they often attempt to place themselves or a friend within the frame, recreating a fictional character's iconic pose (2002, p. 149). This tends not to be the case with Marsili and the members of the *Spaghetti Western Web Board*. Since some of the Spanish filming locations have changed almost beyond recognition, the web board members' photographs tend to act as melancholy records of the sad decline of iconic sites that they have come to appreciate thanks to their affection for Italian Westerns. It would seem clear that the impending sense of loss experienced after viewing Marsili's *C'era una Volta il Western* actually played a part in stimulating the board members' initial trip to Almeria. As such, there is a sense of preservation and conservation about these fans' need to capture visual records of what remains of these sites before displaying the results on websites for future generations to appreciate (see Commes & Yasuda, 2005; Watts, 2004) and this perhaps distinguishes the *Spaghetti Western Web Board* members from other fan communities. By matching the framing and the angles of the scenic photographs that they take to screen grabs taken from Italian Westerns, these fans' web site galleries are able to provide a series of startling 'then and now' comparisons of Almeria's Italian Western filming locations. Doreen Massey has observed that 'no spaces are stable, given for all time; all spaces are transitory and one of the most critical things about spatiality...is that it is always being made' (quoted in Acland, 2003, p. 56). The *Spaghetti Western Web Board* members appear to be acutely aware of this concept.

Conclusion

It is clear that the transnational members of the *Spaghetti Western Web Board* are a virtual community who cross virtual borders in order to gather together on-line. Furthermore, when on-line they are a particularly discursive and active community. The community's activities within the realm of fan cultures make full use of a variety of new technologies. Despite being a community that is built around filmic texts, the *Spaghetti Western Web Board*'s members' attempts to be a self-sufficient fan community can be fruitfully compared to the similarly productive and participatory fan communities that coalesce around cult television texts like *Star Trek* and *The X-Files*. The community's fan culture activities ultimately resulted in a number of them crossing real world borders and travelling to Almeria, Spain in order to meet each other face to face.

The Almeria trip proved to be culturally productive, resulting in the shooting of two fan films. Moreover, it led directly to the web board's members' ongoing interest in finding and preserving on film what remains of the often dilapidated and fast disappearing Spaghetti Western shooting locations and this surely qualifies as a form of preservation and conservation that seemingly makes this fan community unique. This intriguing form of fan culture practice, wherein fan discourse leads to travel experiences which in turn provoke further discourse and further travel, demands more detailed research. Accompanying Marsili and the *Spaghetti Western Web Board* members on a future location-hunting trip to Almeria would undoubtedly be the best way to take such research forward.

Acknowledgements

I would like to thank the members of the *Spaghetti Western Web Board* (who kindly allowed me to record and quote their postings) and Franco Cleef and John Nudge (who both kindly agreed to be interviewed). Thanks also to Professor Paul Cooke, Professor Lance Pettitt and *Language and Intercultural Communication*'s anonymous reviewer (for their helpful comments) and Professor Lucia Nagib (for providing a translation of my abstract).

References

Abercrombie, N., & Longhurst, B. (1998). *Audiences*. London: SAGE.

Acland, C.R. (2003). *Screen traffic: Movies, multiplexes and global culture*. Durham & London: Duke University Press.

August, K. (2006a, January 16). Welcome! [Web log message]. Retrieved October 10, 2006, from http://gliattore.blogspot.com/2006_01_16_gliattore_archive.html

August, K. (2006b). Shoot to kill, Kochmedia Germany serves up Spaghetti Western DVDs. *Westerns All'Italiana*, 66, 37.

Bacon-Smith, C. (1992). *Enterprising women: Television fandom and the creation of popular myth*. Philadelphia: University of Pennsylvania Press.

Bakardjieva, M. (2003). Virtual togetherness: An everyday-life perspective. *Media, Culture and Society*, 25(3), 291–313.

Bakhtin, M. (1984). *Rabelais and his world*. Bloomington: Indiana University Press.

Baym, N. (1998). Talking about soaps: Communication practices in a computer-mediated culture. In C. Harris & A. Alexander (Eds.), *Theorizing fandom: Fans, subculture, and identity* (pp. 111–129). New York: Hampton Press.

Betts, T. (2003). The swingin' doors. *Westerns All'Italiana*, 61, 2.

Billiottet, O., & Perez, C. (1994). In the footsteps of the gunfighters. *Spaghetti Cinema*, 57, 2–42.

Bird, S.E. (2003). *The audience in everyday life*. London: Routledge.

Braithwaite, J. (2003). A trip to Almeria. Retrieved October 10, 2006, from http://website. lineone.net/ ~ braithwaitej/mainsite/overview/trip/trip2.htm

Braithwaite, J. (2004). Almeria 04 – The Spaghetti Western Web Board Re-union. Retrieved October 10, 2006, from http://website.lineone.net/~braithwaitej/mainsite/overview/almeria 04/almeria04-intro.htm

Brooker, W., & Jermyn, D. (2003). The fan audience: Cult texts and community. In W. Brooker & D. Jermyn (Eds.), *The audience studies reader* (pp. 167–169). London: Routledge.

Burnett, R., & Marshall, P.D. (2003). *Web theory: An introduction*. London: Routledge.

Canevari, C. (Director). (1970). *Matalo* [Motion picture]. Italy: Wild East.

de Certeau, M. (1984). *The practice of everyday life*. Berkley: University of California Press.

Commes, M., & Yasuda, Y. (2005). Filming location of Spaghetti Western: Spain. Retrieved October 10, 2006, from http://garringo.cool.ne.jp

Denzin, N.K. (1999). Cybertalk and the method of instances. In S. Jones (Ed.), *Doing internet research* (pp. 107–125). London: SAGE.

Derringdo, (2006, November 4). If your fandom was a nation, what would it be like? [Web log message]. Retrieved November 4, 2006, from http://derringdo.livejournal.com/

Doctor Quinn, Medicine Woman. (1993–1998). [Television series]. United States: Columbia Broadcasting.

Eustace, M. (1995). To Almeria in search of the West, part one. *Spaghetti Cinema*, 61, 31–41.

Fernback, J. (1999). There is a There There. In S. Jones (Ed.), *Doing internet research* (pp. 203–220). London: SAGE.

Frayling, C. (1981). *Spaghetti Westerns: Cowboys and Europeans from Karl May to Sergio Leone*. London: Routledge & Kegan Paul Ltd.

Grant, K. (1997). Showdown in Almeria. *Blood, Money and Vengeance*, 4, 3–8.

Gregory, C. (1997). *Be seeing you: Decoding The Prisoner*. Luton: John Libbey Media.

Hills, M. (2002). *Fan cultures*. London: Routledge.

Hodgkiss, C. (1997). Showdown in Almeria. *Blood, Money and Vengeance*, 4, 8–11.

de la Iglesia, A. (Director). (2002). *800 Bullets* [Motion picture]. Spain: Sogepaq.

Isenberg, R. (Director). (2006a). *Once Upon a Time in the Autumn* [Motion picture]. United States: Independent.

Isenberg, R. (2006b). Back cover sleeve note. *Once Upon a Time in the Autumn*. Private pressing, [DVD-R].

Jenkins, H. (1992). *Textual poachers*. London: Routledge.

Jenkins, H. (2002). Interactive audiences? The 'collective intelligence' of media fans. In H. Jenkins (Ed.) (2006), *Fans, bloggers and gamers: Exploring participatory culture* (pp. 134–151). New York: New York University Press.

Jordan, T. (1999). *Cyberpower: The culture and politics of cyberspace and the internet*. London: Routledge.

Kiral, C. (Director). (2005). *The making of Per un Pugno di Sogni* [Documentary]. Turkey: Leomor Pictures.

Kollock, P., & Smith, M.A. (1999). Communities in cyberspace. In M.A. Smith & P. Kollock (Eds.), *Communities in cyberspace* (pp. 3–25). London: Routledge.

Leone, S. (Director). (1964). *A fistful of dollars* [Motion picture]. Italy: United Artists.

Leone, S. (Director). (1965). *For a few dollars more* [Motion picture]. Italy: United Artists.

Leone, S. (Director). (1966). *The good, the bad and the ugly* [Motion picture]. Italy: United Artists.

Leone, S. (Director). (1968). *Once upon a time in the West* [Motion picture]. Italy: Paramount.

Levy, P. (1997). *Collective intelligence: Mankind's emerging world in cyberspace.* Cambridge: Perseus.

Marsili, M. (Director). (2003). *C'era una Volta il Western* [Motion picture]. Italy: Nighteagle Films.

Marsili, M. (Director). (2004). *Per un Pugno di Sogni* [Motion picture]. Italy: Nighteagle Films.

Pannone, G. (Director). (1998). *L'America a Roma* [Television documentary]. Italy: Intelfilm

The Prisoner. (1967–1968) [Television series]. UK: ITC.

Rheingold, H. (2000). *The virtual community: Homesteading on the electronic frontier* (Rev. ed.). London: The MIT Press.

Seiter, E. (2000). Making distinctions in TV audience research: Case study of a troubling interview. In H. Newcomb (Ed.), *Television: The critical view* (6th ed., pp. 495–518). Oxford: Oxford University Press.

Smith, M. (1992). *Voices from the WELL: The logic of the virtual commons* (unpublished Master's thesis). Department of Sociology, UCLA.

Sollima, S. (Director). (1966). *The big gundown* [Motion picture]. Italy: Columbia Pictures.

Sollima, S. (Director). (1968). *Run, man, run* [Motion picture]. Italy: Blue Underground.

Spaghetti Western Web Board (SWWB). (2006, February 1–2007, January 30). Retrieved February 1, 2006 – January 30, 2007, from http://disc.yourwebapps.com/Indices/160642. html

Spiers, B. (Director). (1984). *A fistful of travellers' cheques* [Television film]. UK: Channel 4.

Squitieri, P. (Director). (1971). *Django challenges Sartana* [Motion picture]. Italy: PAC.

Star Trek (1966–1969) [Television series]. United States: Paramount Television.

Sturges, J. (Director). (1960). *The magnificent seven* [Motion picture]. United States: MGM.

Tuco Tours. (2006, October 10). The Dollars Trilogy experience. Retrieved October 10, 2006, from http://www.tucotours.co.uk/tours.htm

Tulloch, J., & Jenkins, H. (1995). *Science fiction audiences.* London: Routledge.

Urry, J. (2002). *The tourist gaze* (2nd ed). London: SAGE.

Wakefield, S.R. (2001). Your sister in St. Scully: An electronic community of female fans of 'The X-Files'. *Journal of Popular Film & Television, 29*(3), 130–137.

Watts, R. (2004). Sergio Leone Spaghetti Western locations. Retrieved October 10, 2006, from http://www.btinternet.com/~ramon/sw/index.html

Wellman, B., & Gulia, M. (1999). Virtual communities as communities. In M.A. Smith & P. Kollock (Eds.), *Communities in cyberspace* (pp. 167–194). London: Routledge.

The X-Files. (1993–2002). [Television series]. United States: 20th Century Fox Television.

Crossing the intercultural borders into 3rd space culture(s): implications for teacher education in the twenty-first century

Melinda Dooly

Department of Language, Literature and Social Science Education, Faculty of Education, Universitat Autònoma de Barcelona, Barcelona, Spain

This article looks at a year-long network-based exchange between two groups of student-teachers in Spain and the USA, who were involved in various network-based collaborative activities as part of their teaching education. Their online interaction was facilitated through diverse communicative modes such as Skype, Moodle, Voicethread and Second Life (SL). It was found that the participants' interaction with their distanced partners varied according to the available communication modes as they constructed 'membership' identities in the virtual interaction. The analysis hints at the need to reconsider what 'intercultural' means within a 'third space'.

Este artículo analiza un intercambio a través del Internet entre dos grupos de estudiantes de educación (formación de profesorado) de España y los EE.UU. Los alumnos participaron en diversas actividades de 'telecolaboración' como parte de sus cursos de metodología y practicas. Su interacción 'online' fue facilitada a través de diversas modalidades de comunicación, tales como Skype, Moodle, Voicethread y Second Life (SL). El estudio muestra que la interacción entre los participantes variaba según los tipos de comunicación disponibles y esto influía en la manera en que se construyeron sus identidades en la interacción virtual. El análisis apunta a la necesidad de reconsiderar que se entiende por 'intercultural' dentro del 'tercer espacio'.

Introduction

This article outlines and then discusses a year-long network-based exchange between two groups of student-teachers; one group in Catalunya (Spain) and the other group in Illinois (USA). The student-teachers were involved in various collaborative activities; however this text looks principally at the student-teachers' collaborative designing of teaching sequences and podcasts. Their online interaction was facilitated through diverse communicative modes including forums, Skype, Moodle, Voicethread and Second Life (SL).[1] Literature on network exchanges of this type often mentions Intercultural Communicative Competences (ICC) as a key element for success and/or a possible stumbling block for this form of interaction (Belz, 2007; Furstenberg & Levet, 2010; Helm & Guth, 2010; Müller-Hartmann, 2006; O'Dowd, 2006). Along those lines, this paper interrogates what ICC in a 'third space' (Bhabha, 1994) may mean, when placed against the backdrop of computer-mediated communication and virtual communities.

This is especially relevant for the student-teachers in the study, some of whom were quite familiar with these technological tools and virtual spaces, others who were less so.

> Although many millions of people do not have access to the Internet, a computer, or even basic education, a new generation has grown up in a digital age where geographic boundaries do not pose a barrier to international, intercultural communication. As a sub-group, SL participants have moved beyond static web pages and text-based social networking environments, choosing instead to explore the new virtual environments. (Diehl & Prins, 2008, pp. 102–103)

Thus, these student-teachers can easily suppose that their future students will be 'digital natives' (Prensky, 2001) with ample personal experience in using the Internet. Furthermore, no matter what their own personal experience with these tools, most, if not all, of these student-teachers will be expected to integrate some sort of pedagogical use of Web 2.0 into their language classrooms in the future (Dooly, 2010a). Many definitions of what exactly Web 2.0 is have emerged since the term was first coined by O'Reilly in 2005 to refer to the interconnected, globalized world of business.

> In the last few years much hyperbole has surrounded Web 2.0, which for some is just a new technology bubble while for others it is a radical transformation in the way people communicate, socialise, do business (Tapscott and Williams 2006) and do politics (Tumulty 2008; Delany 2008), as seen by the extraordinary role played by social media in Barack Obama's 2008 election campaign for the US presidency or in the organization and reporting of the protests after the 2009 elections in Iran. (Guth & Helm, 2010, p. 15)

The upheaval of the Tunisian government, baptised as the Jasmine revolution (Walt, 2011), can be added to this list of how Web 2.0 is changing the balance of world political power. 'The Jasmine Revolution [...] needed no leaders to rally the protesters or organize the demonstrations. Instead, the revolt was refueled by a steady stream of anonymous text messages, Twitter and Facebook updates' (Walt, 2011). The fact that the Egyptian government declared an immediate blackout of Internet and cellphones on 28 January 2011, as the unrest of Tunisia swept into Egypt less than two weeks after Tunisian President Zine el Abidine Ben Ali fled the country, provides further evidence that heads of state are becoming more aware of the 'viral' power of new communication technology.

It is patent, then, that how student-teachers and their future students use these Web 2.0 tools to communicate with other, distanced partners will be an important issue, not only in political terms but also in the sense of construction of individual and cultural identity. The main idea of network-based language practice (tele-collaborative language learning) is that computers provide a means of mediating communication between persons across the globe, synchronously or asynchronously. The possibilities of language learners coming into contact with other learners or speakers of the target language they are studying have multiplied exponentially with the increment of Internet access in the classroom, not to mention their use of communication technologies in their personal lives.

This means that the opportunities for transglobal contact between language learners from different cultures are also much greater. Nonetheless, social actors coming from different cultural backgrounds (with specific collaborative tasks to undertake) may not necessarily follow the patterns of face-to-face intercultural interaction. It is proposed in this paper that the affordances of the different interactional modes may have rendered 'traditional' categorizations of culture less salient to these student-teachers when engaged in 'emergent' cultures such as virtual communities. It also implies a need to revise current models of ICC and their application to such exchanges.

> Telecollaboration 2.0 situates itself within a globalized context where the concepts of language and culture differ from those associated with national identity. [...] Much of the interaction within this globalized context takes place online where individuals may have multiple identities which may certainly include national and ethnic ones but, as Risager (2007) argues, "identities should be understood as processes that take place between particular players under particular historical and geographical circumstances in multicultural communities that form and develop across existing national boundaries" (p. 1). [...] Within the educational context of Telecollaboration 2.0 projects, the aim is not *necessarily* for learners to prepare to go abroad, but for them to learn to operate, that is to communicate, collaborate, create and negotiate, effectively in multilingual, multicultural global networks using any number of languages [...] and communication modes (oral, visual and/or textual, synchronous or asynchronous) in more or less open or closed environments. (Helm & Guth, 2010, pp. 71–72)

Within a telecollaborative milieu, this article first describes the context and data of the exchange, followed by a discussion of ways in which the individuals oriented their interaction with their distanced partners according to the different available communication channels and modes. The article then looks at how 'membership' identities were constructed in the virtual interaction and the way in which these online identities influenced expectations concerning the behaviour of the 'other'.

How the exchange was set up: context, participants and task-design

The exchange was conceived and implemented as a distanced-partner, triangulated teacher training case study. Making use of various 2.0 tools freely available to the participants, two teacher educators – one at the Universitat Autònoma de Barcelona (UAB), the other located at the University of Illinois Urbana Champaign (UIUC) – designed different tasks and activities for their students to carry out. Three underlying goals of the exchange design were to (a) foster student-teacher reflection on their own practice and to promote applied critical thinking; (b) reduce the feeling of teacher isolation and provide a means of peer-support and knowledge-sharing, as well as opinions and experiences; (c) create a virtual community of practice that these student-teachers might carry over into their professional lives. A key element to the design was the need for collaboration with 'virtual' partners, that is, group members whom the student-teachers could only communicate with through different Internet media.

Locally, the groups of student-teachers were heterogeneous. For instance, in the UAB group there were Spanish, Catalan, Finnish and Czech student-teachers (and one doctoral research student from Cyprus), while in the UIUC group there were North American, Mexican, South Korean, Spanish, Indian and Honduran students. There were more female students than male, with five females and two males in the UAB group and ten females and three males in the UIUC group. The two groups were studying similar degrees but at different levels. The UAB student-teachers were taking part in their school placement tutorials in their final year of Initial Teacher

Training, specializing in English as a Foreign Language; the UIUC students were involved in two specialized courses (Reading and Writing for English as a Second Language and Computer-Mediated Communication (CMC) for ESL Teaching), both at MA level, for a Teaching of English as a Second Language degree.

Some of the challenges faced by the teacher educators when designing the activities involved (a) finding areas of convergence between classes (despite their very different profiles, levels and schedules); (b) designing common tasks that promoted community but did not feel like 'added burden' activities; (c) designing 'sub-tasks' that built up anticipation and a feeling of unity with their online partners before they actually embarked on the real telecollaboration; and (d) dealing with 'divergences' in the programme expectations and outcomes.

Meeting these diverse challenges meant fostering many different types of activities during the year-long exchange. For instance, both groups had completely separate activities related to their face-to-face (henceforth F2F) classes while carrying out telecollaborative activities – some of which were later transferred to their own practice teaching. For reasons of space, this article only discusses some of the telecollaborative activities, in particular two activities that had relevance for both online and F2F collaborative learning.

In the first semester, there was an important point in common. Both classes had to design teaching units (TUs), although even in this case there were divergences: the UAB student-teachers were designing a TU for a foreign language (English) class for primary education, whereas the UIUC student-teachers had to design a CMC-based foreign language (any language; foreign or second language) for either primary or secondary (according to the profile of the student-teacher). In the first semester, then, the teacher-educators decided to limit the online exchange to (a) getting to know each other; (b) forming online working groups; (c) giving feedback on the individual TUs in the working groups. This was facilitated through personal introductions through voicethread, followed by a 'scavenger hunt'[2] in Second Life (see Figure 1 and further explanation in the final notes) where the students not only participated in a general round of introductions of both groups but also got to know their online working partners (unknown to the student-teachers, these groups had already been assigned and they 'ended up' as groups in the scavenger hunt).[3] These same groups were then provided with virtual 'spaces', tools for meetings, and places for displaying and giving feedback for the TUs.

Feedback from the students about the exchange, the different ways in which they made use (or not) of their partners' feedback and the final version of the TUs ended

Figure 1.   UAB and UIUC groups take part in Second Life activities.

the first semester. In the second semester, the teacher-educators felt that it was important to get the network-based partners to truly collaborate on one, unified project per working group. They were also keen to see if the activities online could be more fully integrated into F2F activities. Thus, in the second round of the exchange, the student-teachers were asked to develop together a podcast/vodcast activity[4] that could be used in an F2F teaching situation. Since the UAB students had more opportunities to implement the activity (their school placement was more extensive), the podcasts were designed according to the student needs of the UAB student-teachers.

Post-evaluation (student feedback, triangulated teacher-educators and research student data) revealed that, on the whole, both groups developed more features of reflective teachers in comparison to the beginning of the year. Transcripts and online posts showed more critical thinking about their own and others' teaching practices and beliefs. Moreover, after having lived experiences of a virtual community of practice, the student-teachers had begun to adopt 'ways of doing/being' a teacher (Dooly, 2009) and to engage in the shared repertoire of a community of practice of experienced teachers, displaying more 'experienced practitioner' knowledge, tools, resources and ways of addressing problems than when the exchange had begun. However, it is not the aim of this paper to go into more detail about this aspect of the research (teacher development), which stemmed from the telecollaborative exchange. Instead, the intention is to focus on the notion of Intercultural Communicative Competence (ICC) in 2.0 contexts as the critical nexus of the 3rd space.

Intercultural discursive interaction in 3rd space: a proposal for analysis

It is important to note that despite the international, distanced exchange, Intercultural Communicative Competences were never made explicit as part of the teaching and learning design of the exchange. In part, this was due to the fact that the course programmes themselves were quite limited, and the different activities had already put a considerable 'strain' on the limits that the teacher-educators were allowed in their individual course programmes. Secondly, the teacher-educators were interested to see if issues, questions, or any type of revelation related to interculturality emerged on their own. Considering the heterogeneous composite of the local groups and the fact that the exchange was taking place between two groups on opposite sides of the globe, it seemed almost inevitable that some element of ICC would be made relevant by the participants themselves. After all, the implications of transglobal communication patterns through Web 2.0 seem bound to create intricate and uncertain intercultural interaction, especially when the participating actors all have various cultural backgrounds (Neuliep, 2003).

However, it is important not to 'essentialize' the cultural traits of the participants in the online exchange, since this might lead to assumptions that all incidences or misunderstandings in the exchange were related to the meeting of 'cultures'. It has been suggested that ICC 'is not something innate within us, nor does it occur accidentally' (Wiseman, 2002, p. 211); ICC is 'an acquired quality' (Kupka, Everett, & Wildermuth, 2007, p. 20). This highlights the importance of the context in which the knowledge, skills and attitudes commonly attributed to ICC are attained. If contextualization is coupled with the notion that 'identity' is dynamic and fluid, it becomes apparent that where cultural identity and intercultural competences come into play (e.g. in the 'third space') has a key role in the way in which ICC evolves. Most ICC models designed for language learning have focused on face-to-face encounters. One of the most influential models in language teaching is Byram's model of knowledge of self and other, knowledge of interaction, knowledge of individual and society, skills of interpreting and relating, skills of discovery and social interaction, and attitudes of relativizing self (Byram, 1997). However,

> Byram's model was not developed for telecollaboration contexts where fieldwork, which has "a prospective and retrospective relationship with the classroom" [...], takes place online, and where interaction is not necessarily between native speakers or speakers who have in-depth knowledge of the so-called 'national' target culture. (Helm & Guth, 2010, p. 70)

Furthermore, as Wiseman (2002) has suggested, the agentive role of individuals in any social interaction is important. According to Bourdieu (1977a, 1977b), individuals are 'oriented' to social action and in doing so, they acquire a set of embodied dispositions; nonetheless this should not be understood as previously determined behaviour. An individual's orientation to social action is shaped by social and cultural conditions – which in turn shape and influence their orientation (Dooly, 2010b). In other words, Bourdieu's theory highlights the interrelationship between individual agency and social structures. It is suggested here that the nexus between the two can be observed in the interactants' discursive interaction online.

> Social actors will centre their reasoning, construct further discourse, and act according to seemingly logical, socially and culturally formed discursive practices (Bakhtin 1981, Chouliaraki and Fairclough 1999, Fairclough 1989, 1992, Fairclough 2005, Foucault 1972, Foucault 1980). Of course, as Risse-Kappen (1994) aptly puts it, ideas do not float freely – they cannot exist without agents – but at the same time, these agents are not simply 'carriers' of these ideas, they are social actors engaged in a complex interaction between many different – and sometimes conflictive – discourses and practices. (Dooly, Vallejo, & Unamuno, 2009, p. 5)

Linguists such as Gumperz (1978, 1982) have identified inherent cultural communicative traits. Ethnomethodologists such as Garfinkel and Sacks (1970) carried out ethnographic conversation analysis, based on the assumption that people produce and enact their own individual understanding of social and cultural happenings (interaction) by assigning (constructing) people and objects to categories. This early discourse analysis/ethnographic work has been further developed by researchers in order to identify the ways in which individuals construct and assign cultural categories to groups (Busch, 2010; Dooly, 2009; Hester & Eglin, 1997; Housley & Fitzgerald, 2009; Moermann, 1988).

Thus, the position taken in this paper is that the participants in the telecollaborative exchange were engaged in category-construction (categorizations as fluid memberships), within an action-oriented process. In this ongoing process (e.g. engagement with distanced partners), categories are organized and used in ways that are consequential and implicative for the participants engaged in interaction, both off- and online. This approach allows for the fact that categories will necessarily have fuzzy membership boundaries, and permit multiple and even contrasting possibilities for description. In turn, this allows for an analysis of the talk (face-to-face and online discourse) as a constant dialogic flux composed of both individual and contextual factors.

By recognising talk as a social activity, this language-in-use approach recognises that a category system is not simply for organizing our understanding of the world. Categories are tools for talking about things in ways that are adaptable to the requirements of the situation, adaptable to differences of perspective, and changing perspectives. In short, categories are ways to construct shared meaning. Above all, categories help put utterances to work in the pragmatics of social interaction. [...] It could even be argued that interactive discourse is a situated cognitive activity in itself (see Teasly 1997; Saint-Dizier De Almeida 1998). These arguments underline the fact that categorical descriptions involve the discourse participants' choice and that the speaker is positioned, interested and accountable for how things are described and categorized. (Dooly, 2009, p. 32)

This also implies that the telecollaborative exchange can be analysed through terms of discursive social interactions rather than as idealized, essentialist conceptualizations. In other words, the teachers and student-teachers involved are seen as 'inter-textualized' (Bakhtin, 1981, 1986; Maybin, 2005), interactional social beings who are constantly 'accomplishing meaning' (Garfinkel & Sacks, 1970; Goodwin & Duranti, 1992; Schegloff, 2006; Ten Have, 2002) through categorizations; categorizations which are based on normative assumptions about the topic at hand (Dooly, 2009).

This can be seen in the way in which 'membership' identities are constructed online. Significantly, the membership traits that are made relevant by the student-teachers in their online discourse are based on commonalities that they seem to attribute to the whole group, for instance, 'teacher-identity'. This 'shared' identity of 'teacher' in the virtual community allowed them to form a cohesion that was more important than other possible identities (for instance, exchange student, Korean, mother, wife, brother, etc.). This is clear in the way in which the majority of their online discourse aligns with 'teacher-talk': repertoire, jargon, topic-content, indexicality, etc.

Extract 1:Imogene, cho73, and Ann@; online text chat transcript[5]

Imogene: ok of all the documents, look at SRD II Part 1 and SRD II Part 2
Ann@!: ok Imy
Imogene: the others are just supporting materials, you can look at them if you want, but they're hard to edit
cho73: will you make a detailed lesson plan?
Imogene: yes, I'm far behind you guys in that, mainly because I don't know how to sequence these materials
cho73: do you also in charge of craft? if then you can connect craft and lesson material
Ann@!: but Imy, is your unit based on the grammar-based approach or the topic-based one? or maybe none of them...
Imogene: topic based: animals

This 'shared' teacher culture (similar jargon, topics, etc.) was far more relevant to the participants during synchronous interaction than other available identities which the participants could have deployed. There were few incidences in all of the transcripts where 'offline' identities were made relevant and these took place principally in the personal introductions (voicethreads) where some of the student-teachers mentioned their nationality and/or explained something about their countries of origin. Bearing in mind that the voicethreads constituted asynchronous interaction and that the student-teachers made them as personal introductions with a general audience in mind, this deployment of 'traditional' cultural identities is contextually coherent.

Interestingly, however, these 'identities' were not picked up as part of the synchronous discourse between the participants as far as intrapersonal communication goes. In other words, there was little evidence of information-exchange dealing with these other possible identities; on the whole, if any 'group' identities were constructed they were 'UAB' group and 'UIUC' group (other group as activity partner). The 'other' identity could serve as a way of 'opening up' to their partners in the first encounter (as seen in Extract 2), but this was not the norm – in all of the other transcripts the participants limited themselves to 'standard' greetings (in English) and then moved immediately into the assigned activity. (The group in Extract 2, after beginning with a short 'multilingual' exchange, also went straight to the task.)

Extract 2: Javi, Katherine, Lee; online text chat transcript

> **Javi:** Hi Lee!!!
> **Katherine:** Lee ~ are you in here?
> **Lee:** This window?
> **Katherine:** yes!
> **Javi:** there you go
> **Lee:** yea! Hola Javier!
> **Javi:** Hi girl!!!
> **Lee:** ?Como te vas?
> **Javi:** HAHAHAHAHA muy bien guapa!!!
> **Lee:** Now I just need to learn Catalan!
> **Javi:** hahaha, you should
> **Katherine:** So how are you all doing with the project?
> **Lee:** Not too bad, ya'll?
> **Javi:** well.. not too bad
> **Katherine:** Yeah, I think I'm doing okay–but I have a lot more to work on
> **Lee:** We'll let's talk about yours first, Katherine

Of course, it can be argued that the student-teachers were very task-focused and that the lack of sharing of interpersonal/intercultural information is due to the design and purpose of the exchange itself. However, by acknowledging that these pre-existing parameters are part of the contextual boundaries of the interaction, then the way in which the participants evoke (or not) cultural identity in these circumstances is of interest to the study. How they might react in other circumstances outside of the virtual community of practice (VCoP) would not be applicable to this context-related study.

Still, cultural identities did emerge in the transcripts. However, they were used in reference to their students – in other words, cultural identities were relevant for them (in identifying their students and parents) as part of their shared *teacher* identity.

Extract 3: Imogene, cho73 and Ann@; online text chat transcript

> **Ann@!:** but be careful if they're interested in some topics such as drugs, sex...cause parents may not like that...
> **Imogene:** These are Korean students Anna, not Spaniards!
> **Ann@!:** hahahah

Imogene: just kidding!
cho73: That's interesting point
Imogene: actually Americans would be worse! [. . .]
Ann@!: I only say parents from Barcelone are "beyond protective" [. . .]
cho73: Korean parents will not lose in terms of overprotective..
Imogene: this would be interesting to research

This does not mean that there were no misunderstandings or negative evaluations of the 'other' occurring between the student-teachers. However, the transcripts do not show misunderstandings based on *cultural* expectations so much as *personal* (or working group) expectations of the other, as is evident in Extract 4 and Figure 2. These data come from the final oral reflections in the last face-to-face tutorial and personal reflections in the student-teacher's final version of her ongoing wiki that mapped her progress.

Extract 4: Final F2F tutorial; Caterina, Harold, Natalia, Teacher-Educator

CAT: i liked doing the activity but then/ when the result was completely different so what i have planned that was like why did i do this\
HAR: yeah i think i had the same problem it wa:s_ nice to work with them/ and it was kind of productive but the:n in the end when i asked for some changes they seemed like they didn't care anymore they just wanted to go for a holiday so_ [yeah]
NAT: =yeah
TE: yeah the time was a bit off wasn't i:t

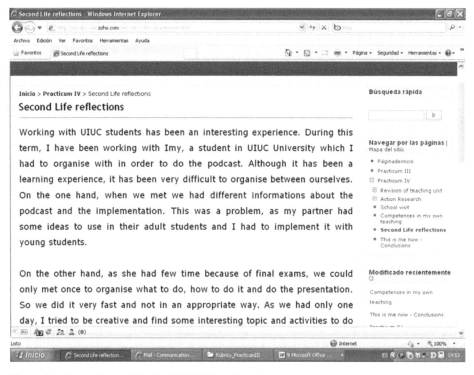

Figure 2.   Screenshot of final wiki (UAB student).

An intercultural 3rd space?

Hinnenkamp (1999) has argued that misunderstanding has become a principal working category for Intercultural Communication studies.

> Generally speaking, [Misunderstandings] MUs have gained the role of a raison-d'être for studying ICC, in particular under the premise that the communication in question is between cultural others, thus transforming MU into intercultural MU. In other studies, conflicts, uncomfortable moments, and miscontextualization in terms of sociocultural knowledge become indicative for ICC. (Hinnenkamp, 1999: para. 1)

The author argues, however, that 'a communicative exchange is not intercultural by virtue of interactants being from different cultural backgrounds. Nor is it intercultural by virtue of a misunderstanding between interactants from different cultural backgrounds' (ibid.). Along these lines, Hinnekamp calls for an interrogation of essentializing misunderstandings as intercultural without taking into consideration the interactional structure. The previous negative evaluations shown in Extract 4 and Figure 2 could be interpreted as a mismatch between different national, ethnic, cultural or linguistic backgrounds (e.g. 'we' Catalan/Spanish group versus 'they' American group); however, given the homogeneous backgrounds of both groups and the fact that national, ethnic or cultural traits were not made relevant previously, this does not seem an appropriate conclusion. Instead, it appears that there is a general disappointment in the online behaviour of some of the *members* of the *virtual community of teachers*. In other words, it appears that this cohesive identity (with all of them as members) was the most relevant one for them and the one that they oriented themselves to.

Does this mean that interactants in virtual communities constitute their intercultural encounters differently? As early as 1998, Poster asked:

> Is virtual ethnicity an alternative to the binaries of particularism and universalism, parochialism, and cosmopolitanism, inserting itself between nations and communities, earthly ethnicities and races? (Poster, 1998, p. 186)

Much has been said about the potential of virtual communities and computer-mediated communication as a means of crossing boundaries and transcending 'real' world identities. At the same time, third space has been used to refer to a space between different cultures, where participants must negotiate cultural differences. Arguably, this space can promote intercultural learning by helping create awareness that one's own perspective on the world is not the only one. However, as Helm and Guth (2010) point out,

> even though there has been much written on the new generation of students, (Prensky 2001, 2009; Oblinger and Oblinger 2005), the fact that students use these tools in their personal spheres does not automatically mean that they are capable of using them for effective learning in inter- and multicultural contexts. (Helm & Guth, 2010, p. 100)

The unfamiliarity of some of the contexts in which students in the exchange were interacting did, at times, seem to make the students more aware of the different possible *channels* of communication. At times, they indicated a lack of familiarity or difficulties with some of the tools, thus they 'switched' to another channel, as in Figure 3. At the same time, when dealing with interaction that was

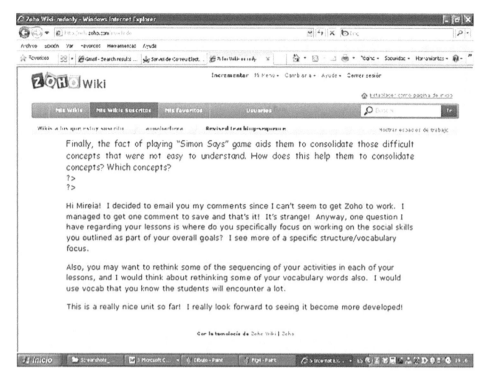

Figure 3.   UAB student's TU and UIUC feedback on Zoho.

more familiar for them (e.g. information exchange through google.docs, text chats), the exchange closely follows a format that is easily transferable (and very similar) to an F2F situation, as in Extract 5.

Extract 5: Nuria, Eunice; online text chat transcript

Nuria: I am learning a lot reading your units in google.docs, the truth is that I didnt know about creative writing or critical reading, thanks! now I understand better with the 2nd draft. i also like they can choose what they want to write and they dont feel pressure or ashamed of beeing read aloud, because is anonimous
eunice: yea i think it'll help them be less biased
Nuria: however I think in your first lesson perhaps you wont be enough time to do what you planned
eunice: right. I think time is an issue.
Nuria: but i dont know your students, perhaps they can do it well
eunice: i'm thinking about stretching the unit to more days

Nonetheless, in distinctly 'new' and unfamiliar environments, such as Second Life, the students expressed fear, reluctance and, at times, even dislike towards the medium of communication (see Figure 4).

Dooly (2010b) proposes a pedagogical model for teaching ICC that combines features of Bourdieu's theory of individuals' socially-oriented social action and embodied dispositions, with Bennett's six stages of intercultural sensitivity and developmental procedures. If this model is used here as a tool for analysis of the

Speaking about the second life experience, I have to admit it has not been a nice experience. I found it unnecessary as it was easier to organise ourselves by messenger or skype than by second life. It is true that it is more personal but it is not worthy as is not a easy tool to deal with. Moreover, my computer was so old that I could not follow the rest of the people when we get together. It was a horrible experience for me. On the contrary, when we did the final party to say good bye was a nice experience as we could be all together exchanging experiences and dancing together.

Figure 4.   Personal reflection in final wiki.

student-teachers' behaviour, it could be argued that the students in the exchange were in ethnorelative positions (e.g. adaptation stage) when dealing with channels of communication online that they were familiar with: they displayed 'behavioural code-shifting' and appeared 'comfortable with crossing points' (Dooly, 2010b, p. 63). However, when faced with unknown modes of communication they were ethnocentric: uncertain of their own agency and how to interact.

Significantly, their feelings towards the new technological tools were remarkably similar to the characteristics outlined by Matsumoto, Leroux, and Yoo (2005) when describing intercultural conflict and misunderstandings: negative emotions that 'are upsetting to our self concepts (…) Uncertainty contributes to this conflict. People may become impatient with or intolerant of the ambiguity, leading to anger, frustration, or resentment' (Matsumoto, Leroux, & Yoo, 2005, p. 16).

Does this imply that the students were involved in a new third space culture that at times made them feel angry, frustrated or resentful? If so, was their discomfort due to the context, the interaction or the interactants? Reasonably, when discussing Intercultural Communication and possible miscommunications, removing the interactants from the picture makes little sense – at least in the 'real' world. However, where does one draw the line about what constitutes a 'real' interactant in a 'virtual' world, when the interaction may take place between an avatar manipulated by a 'real' person and a 'bot' – which is computer-generated but still capable of interacting with the other avatars? Can one say that the student-teacher depicted in Figure 5 has 'integrate[d] fully in multiple environments and able to see [herself] as [a] co-constructor of culture' (Dooly, 2010b, p. 63) – features which Dooly has signalled as necessary for being interculturally competent – even if that only means that the teacher-student has adapted 'to society changes' and learnt to kitesurf in SL?

Furthermore, the data shows that the UAB and UIUC student-teachers achieved rich and meaningful exchanges and sharing of opinions and knowledge in some modes, but in other modes communication was more difficult or the participants felt that they were outside of their 'comfort zone'. Significantly, the same working groups, coming from different cultural backgrounds, at times co-constructed shared identity (e.g. teacher) and breakdowns in communication were minimal and in other moments, in more complex (third world?) environments, some misunderstandings occurred, as is evidenced in Figure 6.

Looking at the interaction from a 'performative' perspective (that takes into account both the context and the interactants) leads to the question: Was the student-teacher frustrated because of an intercultural misunderstanding with her online partner? Was the frustration due to technological issues only? Both participants were engaged in interaction in a 'foreign' culture (Second Life), but it is difficult to determine just how much influence their personal 'real' backgrounds may have had on their 'virtual' interaction. Are these misunderstandings related

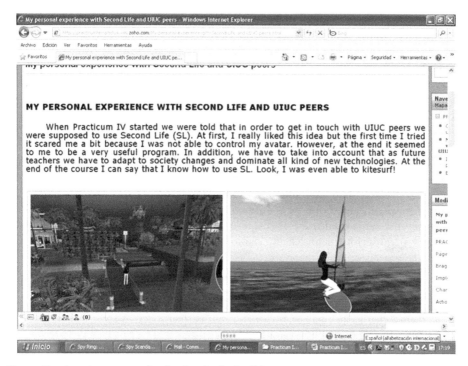

Figure 5.   Another personal reflection in final wiki.

to a new SL culture? Holliday, Hyde, and Kullmann (2004) state that 'any study of culture will inevitably be complex' (p. 64), but what happens when these cultures are 'mixed' with a possible third 2.0 culture?

It seems that the fusing of *Inter*-cultural and *Inter*-net may require new parameters for defining and analysing ICC. Moreover, for teachers working with telecollaborative

---

Printable   Page 1 of 1

Subject	RE: Hi
From	XXXXXXXXXXXX
Date	Friday, April 2, 2010 5:36 pm
To	MelindaAnn.Dooly@uab.cat

Dear Melinda,

I am sorry that I disappeared from SL earlier! I really feel bad and wanted to explain you what happen. When we were all on the scavanger hunt I asked **XXXXX** to help me with my avatar because she really not controllable at all. When we had to find the scooter (which was really cool) I got lost and IM **XXXXX** again. Then I felt **XXXXX** got impatient with me because i noticed it in her voice. I could hear her but she not hear me (my mike was not working). En fin, I become really frustrated and decided to quit. I hope you are not mad at me.

See you in class tomorrow.

Figure 6.   Email to teacher.

language learning environments, they must be aware the students should be 'nudged' beyond their cultural comfort zones into cross-cultural encounters and experiences that promote intercultural literacy (Heyward, 2002), but at the same time 'uncomfortable encounters alone are an insufficient condition for developing intercultural literacy, since they may stimulate learning about oneself and others or reinforce prejudice, nationalism and the like' (Diehl & Prins, 2008, p. 106).

Defining ICC in a third space may seem to be a merely academic question, however, given the growing interest for telecollaboration in language learning the question takes on a more practical hue. The acceptance that ICC should be included in not only general education but language learning is well-documented (Alfred, Byram, & Fleming, 2003; Byram, Gribkova, & Starkey, 2002; Osler & Starkey, 2005; Trujillo Sáez, 2002), but the focus on ICC in 2.0 contexts is still a rather uncharted terrain. Are we talking about 'new' Intercultural Competences for language teachers or are they the same competences disguised in avatar clothing? Consider this short extract of a transcript for an SL interaction.

Extract 6: Transcript from SL: Three female avatars in brainstorming session

> [...] the chapter is so short that I could literally type up the first five or six chapters and send them to her as an email_she's like a _is our partner a her? A she?

As indicated by the extract, the gender of the avatar does not necessarily indicate the gender of the avatar owner in 'real' life. Research on language and gender underscore the socially-constructed aspects of gender (Cameron, 1990; Eckert & McConnell-Ginet, 2003; Norton & Toohey, 2004), suggesting that many male–female variations in use of language features are context-dependent. This implies a need for foreign language teachers' awareness about socio-psychological factors, from a gender perspective, as part and parcel of learner diversity. Moreover, the understanding of the concept of identity has expanded from self to language – through social contexts – into 'moment identification' (Omoniyi, 2006) (although, admittedly, language is not the only means for constructing identity). Inevitably, then, the transgendered possibilities in SL interaction are relevant to teaching pedagogies as they move increasingly towards the integration of 2.0 tools. However, in these 'third space' domains of teaching, it is not only difficult to know discursive partners' cultural identity or gender, they may not even appear as 'human' (see Figure 7).

This implies new communication semiotics – new uses of proxemic markers (e.g. emoticons, images, sounds and even touch are all part of a wide spectrum of communicative practices and competences in Web 2.0 communicative practices). In some cases, communicative practices may mirror 'real life'.

> SL Residents communicate through text, audio and 'gestures', which are scripts that allow users to communicate through body language using particular movements or sounds [...] proximity and placement of avatars and scripted gestures such as nodding 'yes' or 'no', shrugging, or smiling provide visual cues and shape interaction, all of which play a role in intercultural communication competence. (Molinsky et al., 2005; cited in Diehl & Prins, 2008, p. 104)

In other cases, the communicative practices pertain to the 'Internet culture' only. This can carry consequences for language teaching and learning in these new environments as teachers must deal with 'new' formulae for politeness (e.g. the many

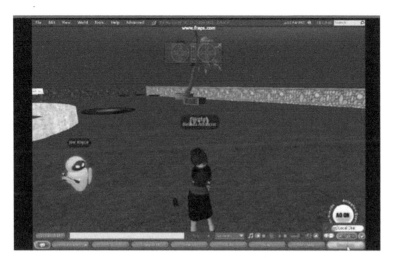

Figure 7.   Interaction with an 'alien' in SL.

disruptions and 'interruptions' that take place in synchronous text and audio chats and interaction in virtual worlds), new ways of discursively establishing topics (e.g. going 'straight to the point' in chats, emails and Instant Messaging) and a new sense of intimacy and sharing of details (e.g. the 'Facebook' culture), just to name a few areas. Kern (2010) argues that communicative competences must take into consideration the different modes by which meaning is mediated, which he has called critical semiotic awareness. Does language learning (and subsequently, language teacher education) also need to consider critical semiotic intercultural awareness? Guth and Helm (2010) propose a three-domain ICC model which considers the operational, cultural and critical dimensions of telecollaborative language learning.

Assuming that a 'third space', constituted through computer-mediated commu-nication, can be exploited for educational purposes, activities can be designed that endeavour to get students (or, as in this case student-teachers) to participate in joint *de*-construction and *re*-construction of shared knowledge and understanding by all the participants, including assumed cultural roles and identities, especially in situations where everything is rendered unfamiliar. The online discursive practice of the student-teachers in this exchange indicates traits associated with an online 'operational attitude: willingness to explore, learn from, participate in, create, and collaborate and share in online communities' (Helm & Guth, 2010, p. 74). Their cultural knowledge (in the sense of a telecollaborative ICC (Helm & Guth, 2010)) is indicative of knowledge of literacy practices applicable to the online contexts they were familiar with. However, the participants were critically aware of 'how and why new information and communication technologies are used' (Helm & Guth, 2010, p. 74) and openly rebuffed suggestions by the teacher educators to use mediums that they felt were not 'useful for me or my future teacher' (UAB student).

Student-teachers also mentioned that they felt that eventually computer-mediated communication modes – especially Second Life – would provide them with possibilities to explore language and cultural learning with their own students, although most of them warned that this was 'far away in the future' (UAB student). Teacher education has a responsibility for orienting student-teachers towards this 'far away future'. Seeing the 'third space' as an opportunity for users to co-create a 'third' culture, through the combination of multiple cultures (including e-cultures), implies that the virtual communities can be where members build a sense of joint enterprise and identity around a specific area of knowledge and activity and share a repertoire of ideas, commitments, memories and ways of doing and approaching things. However, new critical semiotic awareness will be necessary because these 'ways of doing' may no longer be associated with the 'real' world.

Conclusions

This paper has discussed some key issues concerning ICC that have emerged from a case study of an online telecollaborative teacher training programme. The diverse ways in which the student-teacher oriented their interaction with their distanced partners was influenced by their previous knowledge, acceptance, experience and willingness to adapt to the different available communication channels and modes – behaviours and perceptions that often seemed to mimic intercultural interactions in 'real' life. At the same time, the data showed that online interactions between the same group members (all from different cultural backgrounds) varied more according to the modes of communication used than the group member composition. Membership identities were constructed in the virtual interaction in similar ways to membership identities in the face-to-face interactions, especially when dealing with the related practices belonging to the community of teachers. These identities appeared to have more impact on the expectations concerning the behaviour of the 'other' than available social or cultural identities (e.g. information given to their partners in individually designed voicethread presentations).

The analysis of the different types of interaction – through different modes – demonstrates the need for interrogation of essentializing what 'intercultural' means within a space where new means of communication require skills and competences that are not necessarily linked to any specific culture. Following on Kern's (2010) argument that communicative competences must take into consideration the different modes by which meaning is mediated, it is proposed that analysis of such virtual interaction must move beyond ICC towards the notion of critical intercultural semiotic awareness.

Admittedly, the heading of this final section could be considered misleading. Just as the student-teachers in this article expressed, society is changing and there are many new and unknown factors. Given this panorama, it is difficult to draw conclusions. This is an incipient study into the kind of communication and cultures that may emerge through these new modes. It is perhaps too early to say whether these modes can rightfully be called 'third space' and if the interactants, upon entering an e-culture, are transcending and changing the cultural borders of the 'real' world. There needs to be more research into whether the forms of communication in this space do constitute different intercultural communicative competences and, if so, to provide descriptions of precisely what these are.

Acknowledgements

I would like to thank all the wonderful student-teachers who participated in this tele-collaborative exchange. Their enthusiasm for learning has been inspirational. I would also like to thank my telecollaborative teacher-educator partner, Dr Randall Sadler, for his creativity and conviction for all computer-mediated exchanges. Finally, my heartfelt gratitude goes to Dr John O'Regan for all his helpful editing comments on the drafts of this article.

Notes

1. Skype is an audiophony programme that integrates text, voice, and video for communication through phones or the Internet. Moodle (Modular Object-Oriented Dynamic Learning Environment) is an open-source e-learning software platform, or Virtual Learning Environment (VLE). Voicethread is an online platform that allows for collaborative, multimedia slide shows that can be accompanied by audio (other users can comment on the slides with text or voice). Second Life is a three-dimensional online platform where users interact through avatars.
2. This was an activity designed by the teacher trainers for the first meeting of both classes in SL. It was conceived as a means of helping the students learn to 'get around' as avatars on the three EduNation islands (teleporting each other, trying different modes of transport such as walking, riding, or flying), and, at the same time, they could get to know the different individuals through their avatars. Small groups were given assignments to 'find' previously hidden 'acorns' that held further instructions and questions to answer. The questions related to SL (in general), Edunation (geographic spots that they might find useful later on), and the group members (so that they could get to know each other). The information had to be 'delivered' to the teacher trainer avatars at the group's main SL 'hang-out' (where the hunt began).
3. Permission for reproducing participants' online materials was obtained from both study groups before beginning the exchange.
4. Vodcasts (video-on-demand casting) or podcasts are used to create digital content that can be uploaded to a website.
5. Data collected and transcribed by PhD candidate Victoria Antoniadou (Universitat Autònoma de Barcelona).

References

Alfred, G., Byram, M., & Fleming, M. (2003). Introduction. In G. Alfred, M. Byram, & M. Fleming (Eds.), *Intercultural experience and education* (pp. 1–14). Clevedon: Multilingual Matters.

Bakhtin, M. (1981). *The dialogic imagination: Four essays by M.M. Bakhtin* (M. Holquist, Ed., C. Emerson & M. Holquist, Trans.). Austin: University of Texas Press.

Bakhtin, M. (1986). *Speech genres and other late essays* (C. Emerson & M. Holquist, Ed., V.W. McGee, Trans.). Austin: University of Texas Press.

Belz, J.A. (2007). The development of intercultural communicative competence in telecollaborative partnerships. In R. O'Dowd (Ed.), *Online intercultural exchange* (pp. 127–166). Clevedon: Multilingual Matters.

Bhabha, H.K. (1994). *Location of culture*. London and New York, NY: Routledge.

Bourdieu, P. (1977a). Cultural reproduction and social reproduction. In J. Karabel & A.H. Halsey (Eds.), *Power and ideology in education* (pp. 487–511). New York, NY: Oxford University Press.

Bourdieu, P. (1977b). *Outline of a theory of practice* (R. Nice, Trans.). Cambridge: Cambridge University Press.

Busch, D. (2010). Shopping in hospitality: situational constructions of customer-vendor relationships among shopping tourists at a bazaar on the German-Polish border. *Language and Intercultural Communication, 10*(1), 72–89.

Byram, M. (1997). *Teaching and assessing intercultural communicative competence.* Clevedon: Multilingual Matters.

Byram, M., Gribkova, B., & Starkey, H. (Eds.). (2002). *Developing the intercultural dimension in language teaching: A practical introduction for teachers.* Strasbourg: Council of Europe, Language Policy Division.

Cameron, D. (1990). *Feminism and linguistic theory* (2nd ed.). London: Macmillan.

Diehl, W.C., & Prins, E. (2008). Unintended outcomes in second life: Intercultural literacy and cultural identity in a virtual world. *Language and Intercultural Communication, 8*(2), 101–118.

Dooly, M. (2009). *Doing diversity: Teachers' construction of their classroom reality.* Bern: Peter Lang.

Dooly, M. (2010a). Teacher 2.0. In S. Guth & F. Helm (Eds.), *Telecollaboration 2.0. Language, literacies and intercultural learning in the 21ˢᵗ century* (pp. 277–303). Bern: Peter Lang.

Dooly, M. (2010b). Shopping across the (EU) market: Teacher trainees look for experience abroad. *Language and Intercultural Communication, 10*(1), 54–71.

Dooly, M., Vallejo, C., & Unamuno, V. (2009). *Linguistic Minorities Thematic Report. EPASI in Europe (Charting Educational Policies to Address Social Inequalities in Europe). European Commission Report.* London: Institute for Policy Studies in Education.

Eckert, P., & McConnell-Ginet, S. (2003). *Language and gender.* New York, NY: Cambridge University Press.

Garfinkel, H., & Sacks, H. (1970). On formal structures of practical action. In J.C. McKinney & E.A. Tiryakian (Eds.), *Theoretical sociology: perspectives and developments* (pp. 338–366). New York, NY: Appleton-Century-Crofts.

Goodwin, C., & Duranti, A. (1992). Rethinking context: An introduction. In A. Duranti & C. Goodwin (Eds.), *Rethinking context* (pp. 1–42). Cambridge: Cambridge University Press.

Gumperz, J.J. (1978). The conversational analysis of interethnic communication. In E.L. Ross (Ed.), *Interethnic communication,* (pp. 13–31). Athens: The University of Georgia Press.

Gumperz, J.J. (1982). *Discourse strategies.* Cambridge: Cambridge University Press.

Furstenberg, G., & Levet, S. (2010). Integrating telecollaboration into the language classroom: Some insights. In S. Guth & F. Helm (Eds.), *Telecollaboration 2.0. Language, literacies and intercultural learning in the 21ˢᵗ century* (pp. 305–336). Bern: Peter Lang.

Guth, S., & Helm, F. (2010). Introduction. In S. Guth & F. Helm (Eds.), *Telecollaboration 2.0. Language, literacies and intercultural learning in the 21ˢᵗ century* (pp. 13–35). Bern: Peter Lang.

Helm, F., & Guth, S. (2010). The multifarious goals of telecollaboration 2.0: Theoretical and practical implications. In S. Guth & F. Helm (Eds.), *Telecollaboration 2.0. Language, literacies and intercultural learning in the 21st century* (pp. 69–106). Bern: Peter Lang.

Hester, S., & Eglin, P. (1997). Membership categorization analysis: An introduction. In S. Hester & P. Eglin (Eds.), *Culture in action. Studies in membership categorization analysis* (pp. 1–23). Washington, DC: International Institute for Ethnomethodology and Conversation Analysis & University Press of America.

Heyward, M. (2002). From international to intercultural: Redefining the international school for a globalized world. *Journal of Research in International Education, 1*(1), 9–32.

Hinnenkamp, V. (1999). The notion of misunderstanding in intercultural communication. *Journal of Intercultural Communication* [online journal], *1*. Retrieved January 7, 2011, from http://www.immi.se/jicc/index.php/jicc/article/view/163/130

Holliday, A., Hyde, M., & Kullmann, J. (2004). *Intercultural communication: An advanced resource book.* London: Routledge.

Housley, W., & Fitzgerald, R. (2009). Membership categorization, culture and norms in action. *Discourse & Society, 20*(3), 345–362.

Kern, R. (2010, May). *Textualization and Recontextualization: How Electronically-Mediated Communication Can Contribute to Critical Semiotic Awareness.* Paper presented at the

Eurocall Teacher Education SIG Workshop 2010, Institut National de Recherche Pédagogique (INRP), Lyon, France.

Kupka, B., Everett, A., & Wildermuth, S. (2007). The rainbow model of intercultural communication competence: A review and extension of existing research. *Intercultural Communication Studies, XVI*(2), 18–36.

Matsumoto, D., Leroux, J., & Yoo, S.-H. (2005). Emotion and intercultural communication. *Kwansei Gakuin University Journal, 99*, 15–38.

Maybin, J. (2005, September). *'Speech genres' and 'evaluation' in socialisation and identity: Older children's language practices.* Paper presented at Linguistic Ethnography Forum, Seminar on 'Bakhtin, Language and Discourse', King's College London.

Moermann, M. (1988). *Talking culture. Ethnography and conversation analysis.* Philadelphia: University of Pennsylvania Press.

Müller-Hartmann, A. (2006). Learning how to teach intercultural communicative competence via telecollaboration: A model for language teacher education. In J.A. Belz & S.L. Thorne (Eds.), *Internet-mediated Intercultural Foreign Language Education* (pp. 63–84). Boston, MA: Thomson Heinle.

Neuliep, J.W. (2003). *Intercultural communication: A contextual approach* (2nd ed.). Boston, MA: Houghton Miffling.

Norton, B. & Toohey, K. (Eds.). (2004). *Critical pedagogies and language learning.* Cambridge: Cambridge University Press.

Omoniyi, T. (2006). Hierachy of identities. In T. Omoniyi & G. White (Eds.), *The sociolinguistics of identities* (pp. 11–33). London: Continuum.

O'Dowd, R. (2006). *Telecollaboration and the development of intercultural communicative competence.* Berlin: Langenscheidt.

O'Reilly, T. (2005, September 30). What Is web 2.0: Design patterns and business models for the next generation of software. Retrieved January 29, 2011, fromhttp://www.oreillynet.com/pub/a/oreilly/tim/news/2005/09/30/what-is-web-20.html?page=1

Osler, A. & Starkey, H. (Eds.). (2005). *Citizenship and language learning: International perspectives.* Stoke-on-Trent: Trentham Books.

Poster, M. (1998). Virtual ethnicity: Tribal identity in an age of global communications. In S. Jones (Ed.), *Cybersociety 2.0: Revisiting computer-mediated communication and community* (pp. 184–211). London: Sage.

Prensky, M. (2001). Digital natives, digital immigrants. *On the Horizon, 9*(5), 1–6.

Schegloff, E.A. (2006). Interaction: The infrastructure for social institutions, the natural ecological niche for language, and the arena in which culture is enacted. In N.J. Enfield & S.C. Levinson (Eds.), *Roots of human society* (pp. 70–96). Oxford: Berg.

Ten Have, P. (2002). The notion of member is the heart of the matter: On the role of membership knowledge in ethnomethodological inquiry. *Forum Qualitative Sozialforschung / Forum: Qualitative Social Research, 3*(3), 1–19.

Trujillo Sáez, F. (2002). Towards interculturality through language teaching: argumentative discourse. *Cauce, 25*, 103–120.

Walt, V. (2011, January 31). Tunisia's Nervous Neighbors Watch the Jasmine Revolution. *Time Magazine.*

Wiseman, R.L. (2002). Intercultural communication competence. In W.B. Gudykunst & B. Mody (Eds.) *Handbook of international and intercultural communication* (2nd ed., pp. 207–224). Thousand Oaks, CA: Sage.

Figuring home: the role of commodities in the transnational experience

Christine Penman and Maktoba Omar

School of Marketing, Tourism & Languages, Edinburgh Napier University, Craiglockhart Campus, Edinburgh, EH14 1DJ, UK

This article proposes to investigate the role played by material goods in the transnational experience. Previous research has shown that the movement of people across the world comes with a corollary of cultural flows which find their expression in multiple ways. This article looks more specifically at the kind of commodities that international students bring from home when living in the UK. Informed by interdisciplinary research, it reports on a quantitative study with some qualitative elements investigating the motivation for bringing specific goods, and the nature of those goods. It also looks at the issue of authenticity of provision for the sample by interrogating the importance of the locating process.

Cet article se propose d'examiner le rôle que jouent les biens matériels dans l'expérience transnationale. D'autres recherches ont préalablement démontré que les déplacements humains à travers le monde s'accompagnent de mouvements culturels qui se révèlent de façons multiples. Cet article se penche plus particulièrement sur le type de biens que les étudiants venus de l'étranger apportent de chez eux lorsqu'ils viennent résider au Royaume-Uni. Sous-tendu par des recherches interdisciplinaires, il fait état d'une étude quantitative étayée par des éléments de recherche qualitative qui examine ce qui motive ces étudiants à sélectionner et à transporter certains biens spécifiques ainsi que la nature de ces objets. L'article se penche également sur la question d'authenticité en interrogeant l'importance du processus de localisation des objets sélectionnés.

Introduction

Cross-cultural studies focus largely on social interactions and interpersonal communication between individuals. Monceri (2009, p. 50) argues that 'identity can and does change trans-culturally and inter-culturally, being the outcome of the concrete interactions taking place between concrete individuals who are situated in different cultural contexts'. This article proposes to take the investigation of the 'concrete' further by looking at another paradigm, namely the non-verbal information mediated through people's relationship to goods when they are in transit between cultures. As such it is not the study of a form of deliberate communication but rather the documenting of relationships between people and inanimate objects which provides an emic perspective on cultural flows. The diegetic approach is through consideration of relevant writing with a cross-disciplinary perspective and description and discussion of empirical research.

As this study brings together human attachment in relation to tangible goods against a background of transnational displacement and emplacement, the research literature which informs it lies at the intersection of a number of fields: in particular, anthropology, sociology, psychology, philosophy, human geography, studies in intercultural communication, marketing and consumer behaviour have relevant contributions to make to our understanding of what people select to take with them when they leave their usual surroundings to move to a different country. The focus of the literature considered is on the cross-fertilisation between social sciences and business-orientated studies both in terms of content and research methodologies, with an emphasis on psychological and sociocultural investigations undertaken for a better understanding of the marketplace.

The paper will first provide an overview of three key themes salient in relevant cross-disciplinary literature: one, crisscrossed by consumer research, sociology and intercultural communication revolves around concepts of identity in relation to consumption and possession; a second body of literature focuses on the conative perception of goods, on a blend of knowledge and affect explored in consumer research and psychology; the third area, dominated by human geography, examines the globalisation and localised patterns of commercial cultures. The thread between these three areas is that of establishing connections between the self and material goods.

We will then move on to report on the empirical research undertaken to provide a modicum of answers to two questions: what kind of commodities do international students travelling to the UK bring from home? And, what role(s) do these commodities fulfil in the transnational experience? Findings will be discussed in relation to theoretical and pragmatic insights offered by the literature.

Goods as informants

In the next three following sections we will consider theoretical contributions to our understanding of the relationships entertained between individuals and their material possessions. The spatial paradigm establishes a connective strand between the bodies of literature considered.

Identity and consumption

Insights from sociology which widely draws from the informative properties of objects to document the human take on the world are frequently sought by researchers intent on gaining a better understanding of the relationship between consumers and the material world, in particular when those inanimate objects are 'stripped of commodity status' (Epp & Price, 2010) and endowed with personal meaning. Thus Bourdieu's construct of *habitus* conflates the material, spatial and social spheres whereby objects do not just provide background staging but a transactional way of experiencing the world. Regular exposure to a specific range of material goods, selection of some and exclusion of others due to sociocultural considerations feed into and comfort the set of acquired dispositions attached to each individual. In Bourdieu's construct, these internalised values can evolve but remain connected to existing social practices (Bourdieu, 1977). *Habitus* is firmly rooted in a space-, culture- and time-related context. Likewise, space is used metaphorically in consumer research by Belk (1990, p. 669), who looks at the way material possessions add multi-dimensional relief to the notion of core self which in the process emerges as an extended self:

> The notion of the extended self suggests that we transcend the immediate confines of our bodies by incorporating into our identities, objects from our physical environment (Belk 1988). This conception implies that the self is spatially enlarged by such extensions; that our possessions make us bigger people.

If the importance of material objects in the life of individuals is not debatable, the notion of 'core' self which is at the root of Belk's concept of the 'extended self' is seen as more problematic by Ahuvia (2005) as it posits stability and universality. The latter explores further the metaphor used by Belk and through a series of empirical studies comes to the conclusion that in the course of their lives people look for consumption 'solutions' for identity conflicts (for example when torn between an attachment to the past and a predilection for modernity). They opt in particular for demarcating and compromising solutions which allow them to preserve some kind of coherence in their consuming experience. For Ahuvia, this view is pitched against the concept of a postmodern fragmented self which envisions identity as a black hole fed by an endless stream of non-unified and dispirited consumption episodes, such as construed by the American psychologist Cushman (1990). In consumer research Rojas Gaviria and Bluemelhuber (2010) go very much along the same lines as Ahuvia. Turning to the explanatory powers of philosophy and neurobiology to shed light on the symbolic aspects of consumption, they see the past–future timeline as a continuum, and place the search for coherence, which they term 'autobiographical concern', at the heart of the human experience. They base this search for coherence on the philosophical concept of 'desire assemblage' developed by Deleuze who sought to stress the connection between desire for an object with a particular context. Consumption is therefore interpreted as a form of compensation which enables people to carry parts of their past. In the process this allows for elements of stability in times of life role transitions while 'autobiographical concern' allows for multiple interconnections between self, memories and objects.

The commodities and other material possessions that 'translocated' individuals (Appadurai 1996 as cited by Conradson & McKay, 2007, p. 168) select to take with them are part of their biographies. As such they correspond to the notion of 'cultural marker' identified by Holliday (2010, p. 176) as 'an artefact which signifies a cultural reality'. We shall now look in more detail at marketing-led literature on the link between goods endowed with personal value and the locating process of this reification.

Perception of significant material goods

A number of studies investigating human relationships with cherished possessions and more generally with objects and goods selected for consumption adopt or refer to a semiotic approach to interpret the active construction of that aspect of social reality (Davies & Fitchett, 2004; Grayson & Shulman, 2000; Kessous & Roux, 2008; Schembri, Merrilees, & Kristiansen, 2010). Out of the three modes of relationship between the sign vehicle and the signified in the triadic model of the sign in Peircean semiotics – symbolic, iconic and indexical – the indexical mode seems the most potent for an investigation of the link between object, subject and origin as a direct connection or co-occurrence is entailed to release meaning as 'an indexical sign is "like a fragment torn away from the object"' (Pierce as cited by Chandler, 2002, p. 42).

As illustrated in Figure 1 below, powerful relational strands to objects and commodities are fed from the Peircean notion of indexical anchoring as several bodies of research into attachment, nostalgia and the search for product authenticity commonly hark back to a locating process. Thus for Grayson and Shulman (2000) the reasons why people value particular objects and see some of those are irreplaceable stem partly from the fact that irreplaceable possessions are indices: beyond their intrinsic qualities, such as functionality or aesthetic value, 'they have a factual, spatial connection with the special events and people they represent' (Grayson & Schulman, 2000, p. 19). These authors also see 'contamination' between inanimate objects whereby 'possessions may gain value via spatial proximity' (Grayson & Schulman, 2000, p. 19). Although the prosody of the term 'contamina-tion' is arguably generally not positive (as akin to 'corruption'), it is to be interpreted here as a process of partial identification with a context which allows the sought release of memories. The empirical data from the above-quoted study enabled its authors to establish that there is a strong correlation between a personal evaluation of irreplaceability and corporal or temporal indexicality with variations with age and gender. They also established from their study that corporal indexing (i.e. association with particular individuals) tends to become more prominent over time. This body of research is situated within the context of loss of authenticity in society, a fact used by marketers to promote pseudo-authentic products, and described as 'hyper reality' by Baudrillard (1981). Although most of the objects mentioned in this study were mass-produced, the authors come to the conclusion that 'consumers can use commodities to indexically anchor their experiences to the real world' (Baudrillard, 1981, p. 28). Further exploration of this aspect is provided by Schembri et al. (2010) who investigate how brand consumption contributes to the construction of the self. Highlighting the fact that 'while an iconic interrelationship is described as aspirational, an indexical interrelationship is considered historical in nature, linked to past consumption experiences' (Schembri et al., 2010, p. 633). This has

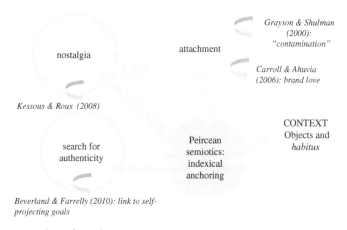

Figure 1. Perception of goods.

implications for the marketplace and in particular for the marketing of brands which can tap successfully into 'the experiential meaning that brands have for consumers in constructing the self' (Schembri et al., 2010, p. 633).

Research on attachment to goods has also turned its attention to the intensity of feeling experienced and the development of a dialectical relationship between consumers and the consumed. Thus Ahuvia (2005) makes the reflection that the word 'love' is used as much in relation to objects and activities as with people. In a subsequent article, Carroll and Ahuvia (2006) point out that 'brand love' is conceptually different from brand liking as it is embedded in the consumers' self-identity. It is not just a more intense form of liking as it bears no graduation (i.e. there is either love or no love) and the intensity of feeling is concomitant with the potential of a brand for a form of self-expression.

Past consumption experiences and their bearing on subsequent material encounters are also core to an investigation of nostalgia as a motivational force. In that interpretative stance, the experiential meaning of goods is linked to a turn to the past and compensation for a form of loss (Holbrook & Schindler, 2003). Nostalgic value placed on particular products hinges on the role of temporal distance but spatial and/or social referents can also play an important part. In a semiotic analysis of nostalgia in relation to products and brands, Kessoux and Roux (2008) established distinction between products which evoke continuity, everyday past (through a layering process, also termed 'long-standing nostalgia'), tradition (through mediation) and those more specifically connected to disruption and a more specific set of circumstances (dissociated from a layering process). They allocated in turn different product types susceptible to be associated to the above categories: in particular, food brands in relation to continuous exposure which is habit-inducing, perfume as a marker of transition and expression of self-concept, jewellery for its associations with an event of unique importance. Their empirical study is located in a particular spatial and cultural frame (French respondents in 2005/2006) but it posits four non-essentialist propositions which link personal traits to a propensity to reach for differentiated triggers of nostalgic feelings. In particular, the authors propose that an attachment to food brands may be commensurate to attachment to the everyday past whereas the symbolic aspect of objects is brought to the fore when individuals see them as material markers of significant life events.

Indexical anchoring is equally very much in the background of studies on the search for authenticity in consumption. In particular, Beverland and Farrelly (2010) build their research on the premise that 'there is widespread agreement that authenticity is a socially constructed interpretation of the essence of what is observed than properties inherent in an object' (Beverland & Farrelly, 2010, p. 839) and bring out three salient themes in the accounts of authenticity drawn from a series of interviews. While two of those themes ('feeling in control' and 'feeling virtuous') revolve around the self, the third, 'feeling connected to people and community', firmly places the locus of perception on situated relationships. The search for authenticity is thereby associated with the attainment of self-projecting gaols which 'involves taking personal ownership of experiences, thus giving objects, brands and/or events an indexical character' (Beverland & Farrelly, 2010, p. 854). This statement on authenticity very much echoes above quoted citations on perception of the irreplaceable and brand love, which suggests that these notions are intimately interwoven through personal contextual reference.

Commodity culture and the transnational experience

Human geographers have pointed to the informative properties of 'traffic in things' (Crang, Dwyer, & Jackson, 2003, p. 446) to document increasingly complex patterns of migrations and forms of settlement, and the cultural interconnections which stretch across the world. Commodity is therefore a 'particular powerful lens through which to see the many dimensions of transnationality' (Crang et al., 2003, p. 451), one which can reflect and distinguish between a great variety of experiences, ranging from impoverished migrant populations to more affluent and privileged groups. This lens does not take heed of national boundaries just as 'cultural identities are no longer clearly wedded to particular nation states' (Crang et al., 2003, p. 439). And in the same way, looking at conceptions of identity in relation to place, Conradson and McKay (2007, p. 168) describe 'the multiply-located senses of self among those who inhabit transnational social fields' and remark that the affiliations and the maintenance of these may be materially and emotionally intensive. This reflection points to the potential of goods and personal possessions to provide both a sense of emplacement and connection to the place of origin. Davies and Fitchett (2004) point out in turn that in the global market place there are places which are less culturally differentiated from others (for instance, airport malls and shopping piazzas) but argue that, from evidence, 'contemporary consumer societies simultaneously retain transnational, national and regional cultural characteristics, as do their consumers' (Davies & Fitchett, 2004, p. 316). However, there is no homogeneity to be found in either the cultural place at the point of departure or at the point of arrival. Therefore consumption patterns are also highly heterogeneous among populations in transition with experiential patterns of acculturation mapping out onto 'forms of symbolic, emotional and functional fracture' (Davies & Fitchett, 2004, p. 328). These differentiated adaptive orientations manifest themselves in turn in the type and number of personal possessions that visitors take along with them.

The study

Research design

The empirical material collected for the purpose of this study originated from a mixed-method approach combining quantitative and qualitative data to develop complementarity between the lines of enquiry (Davies & Fitchett, 2002). A quantitative survey was undertaken in 2010 among non-British undergraduates attending a UK university. Approval from the University Research Ethics Committee was sought and obtained and the anonymity of the respondents guaranteed.

A total of 108 semi-quantitative questionnaires were collected. Beyond general demographic information, initial questions probing general behaviour attracted dichotomous yes/no answers (on whether the respondents brought goods back from home, missed particular brands, felt they could generally source equivalent products from home in the UK, or had noticed any change in their practices). Each of these were followed by questions with response categories allowing multiple answers (e.g. investigating reasons for bringing goods back from home, types of goods brought back, and the locating processes in the search for equivalents) and questions prompting worded responses (comments on favourite items and changing patterns in locating process). All qualitative answers were coded in order to allow for the identification of emergent themes. This data collection was complemented by semi-structured interviews with volunteers which probed some of the issues arising from the survey.

Basic profiling information

Among the initial questions collecting basic demographic data, the respondents were asked to indicate which part of the world they considered their place of origin. This elicited the mention of 24 origins which for the statistical analysis were profiled into four macro geographical groupings: Africa, the Americas, Asia and Europe. In terms of gender, 30% of the respondents were males, 70% females. Most of them (89.2%) had been in the UK for less than 3 years, 63.7% under a year and 5.59% between 1 and 3 years. Most of the respondents who volunteered their age (100 out of 108) were in the 20–30 age groups (88%) while 8.4% were less than 20 and 2.8 between 30 and 40 years of age.

Statistical analysis

For the statistical analysis a Chi-square test was used to establish whether there was a significant difference between expected and actual frequency in the pairing of answers of one type of questions with answers provided in another set.[1] This type of statistical analysis allowed going beyond classification of information under simple paradigms such as geographical origin as it allowed the exploration of relationships between specific types of behaviour. It therefore offered more insight into the experiential side of consumption among students in cultural transition. Qualitative data was elicited from the 25 participants who had volunteered to be contacted in follow-up research from the questionnaires. This is used in the following sections to illuminate some aspects of the findings brought out from the survey.

Findings and discussion

Reasons invoked for bringing back items from home

Among the 108 respondents, only six individuals indicated that they did not bring goods from home. This limited negative response was correlated to a mix of explanations: while three invoked the homogeneity of provision between home and the UK, two asserted the importance of experiencing some goods in their home setting (one respondent through the tautological parallelism 'Scotland is Scotland, Germany is Germany'). Another two invoked pragmatic constraints but subsequently mentioned missing particular items.

The vast majority however (94%) indicated that they did indeed travel to the UK with a selection of goods from home. They invoked the following non-mutually exclusive reasons for doing so: no proper equivalent (54%), value for money (40%), memories from home (39%), perception of quality (29%) and problems of comprehension (6%). These point to a mix of pragmatic and emotive rationales.

It can be argued that there is a degree of overlap between two of these categories, 'memories from home' and 'no proper equivalents', as both use origin of provision and earlier consuming experiences as a benchmark in the host environment (in fact 22% of the respondents ticked both answers). It seems reasonable to assume that the verdict 'no equivalent' is in some cases attributable to very pragmatic reasons.

However, there can also be an implicit reference to familiarity of use and authenticity with an emphasis on conformity to perceptions of the genuine. This insight is corroborated by the list of items cited as examples in the questionnaire, impromptu comments to elaborate on the distinctiveness of these items from a personal viewpoint (e.g. 'I am used to these products so it's hard to live daily without them'; 'to feel home anywhere') and from comments elicited from the unstructured interviews. For instance, when specifically asked to comment on the distinctiveness of the two aforementioned categories, one of the interviewees initially commented that 'no equivalents' was in her mind related to quality and brands rather than to memories. However, subsequent elaboration on this point brought out remarks about the importance of association with familiar places in her home culture:

> Well it has personal value because I feel more confident eating something that I am bringing from home and that I have been consuming all my life than just buying in a random supermarket here and . . . it gives me that sense of security that . . . what I am going to be consuming is going to be . . . you know . . . as it has always been.

This can be related to the previously cited study from Beverland and Farrelly (2010) which predicates the search for authenticity to three personal goals, one being the need to establish connections to people and community. The above quotation clearly establishes that connection. The expression of emotional attachment is also patent. Ahuvia (2005) puts forward the argument that life narratives are built upon conflict and resolution of identity conflicts and that relationships with objects enter in these composites. He points out that in everyday transactions, compromises are rife. However, this is more rarely the case for objects of love as 'loved items feel right; they are not common compromises that satisfice' (Ahuvia, 2005, p. 181). The dismissal of 'proper equivalents' can therefore be seen as a refusal to compromise with less than wholeness.

Types of items brought back

The five categories most commonly mentioned in the sample were, in decreasing order: food (62%), technology (48%), literature (books, magazines, newspapers: 42%), music (37%) and toiletries (37%). The other categories listed in the questionnaire (drinks, music, clothes, housekeeping products, furnishings and others) elicited much lower levels of responses but under 'others' medicines and tobacco featured a few times.

Food

It comes as no surprise that food should feature among the most readily listed items given their potential for a high cultural imprint, often associated with regional and national cultures. It is strongly connected to *habitus* and the social construction of taste. As Askegaard and Madsen (1998, p. 564) comment, food cultures run deep and 'the globalizing tendencies may be considered surface ripples in more deeply rooted cultural patterns'. In the field of consumer behaviour De Mooij (2010, p. 8) makes the same point on the connective strand between food, culture and time:

> Generally speaking, the older the product category, the stronger the influence of culture. This explains why consumption of food products is persistently culture bound.

Food brands have also been found to be often associated with nostalgia, with rooting in the past (Kessous & Roux, 2008).

The statistical analysis in our study established a significant relationship between the fact of bringing food from home and, on one hand, the thought of not being able to find any proper equivalent in this country ($\chi^2 = 11.803$, $df = 1$, $p = 0.001$) and, on the other hand, the practice of going to specialist shops to purchase goods from home ($\chi^2 = 4.525$, $df = 1$, $p = 0.033$). These responses originated from students across the geographical spectrum.

Most brands listed in the questionnaire were food brands with a high preponderance of comfort food (bread, snacks and confectioneries), flavours and spices ('it's essential for a good meal') or brands with a strong cultural heritage (e.g. Lu biscuits, Milleret cheese, Ricard alcohol, Dr Oetker dessert preparations, Milka and Cola Cao chocolate, Jiff peanut butter, Solis tomato sauce, Heng Shun vinegar). The words 'taste' and 'tasty' were recurrently used in synoptic explanations for selecting those items.

For international students, food reminiscent of home (either brought in or purchased in the UK) is a way to anchor their cultural identity in the midst of change and derive 'emotional sustenance' (Brown, 2009, p. 47) which can raise certain items to the status of 'love objects' (Brown, 2009, p. 47). Food has the ability to release memory through 'located texture' (Tolia-Kelly, 2004, p. 326), as testified by a student commenting on the reasons why she takes a ubiquitous item, lentils, from Spain to the UK:

> my lentils I cook them as my mum and my grand mum do ... so with the lentils here I cannot do that ... so I bring them from home and prepare them in their way so it is like being at home

The same student had previously elaborated on the comforting properties of food and the ability for a specific food item – Spanish *jamón* (cured ham) – to establish metonymically a node of connections between sensorial pleasure, cultural belonging and well-being:

> [student] ... because it is ours ... it is Spanish and for example if you are at home and ... if you feel homesick, if you get like some ham and some tomato and some bread, you can make a proper ....
> [researcher] *bocadillo?*[2]
> [student] Yes! So that it makes you feel more ... more like home

Spanish *jamón* is thus in the same league of evocative conduit as Proust's *madeleines*.

Technology

In contrast to the food category, indication of import of technological items was not associated with any further comments in the survey, either about makes and brands or elaborations on personal significance. This may be because of a propensity to be associated with what Carrier (1990, p. 581) terms 'anonymous and fungible commodities', although attachment to high-tech brands and their potential for self-expression is also well documented (Wang & Datta, 2010).

Survey results indicated that if the respondents had been in the country under a year, they were more likely to have brought technology with them ($\chi^2 = 10.285$, $df = 4$, $p = 0.36$). This could be due to a mix of pragmatic reasons (for instance, rapid product obsolescence, identification of sourcing in the UK) and relational issues (related for instance to financing by family) which could be investigated further.

Literature (books and printed press)

This product group yielded two significant associations in the survey: one linking the fact of bringing literature and the European group ($\chi^2 = 8.228$, $df = 3$, $p = 0.042$); the other pointing to a strong relationship between the fact of bringing literature and memories from home ($\chi^2 = 17.498$, $df = 1$, $p = .001$). The only specific comment made was about the lack of individual magazine titles.

It is worth pointing out that 'better of understanding of instructions' was dismissed as a reason for importing these items, which seems to discard linguistic barriers and privileging a sense of connection with language and home culture.

Music

The sample results yielded a significant relationship between the fact of taking music and its ability to evoke memories from home ($\chi^2 = 11.167$, $df = 1$, $p = .001$). This information was not elaborated on by any further comments, but one of the students interviewed pointed out the ease of access to digital sources.

Toiletries

Grooming products, along with clothing, are associated with cathexis, the emotional, psychosexual energy channelled onto an object or idea (Ahuvia, 2005). In a study on 'brand love', Carroll and Ahuvia (2006) concluded that hedonic products tend to attract stronger emotional responses than utilitarian ones and that complex relationships are developed between those products and brand loyalty. In our study, toiletries were the second group of items to be mentioned by brand name. These encompassed brands of personal hygiene products, cosmetics, body creams and lotions. Parallel comments were about the inability to locate the same product, quality and price, and about differences in availability of product range (to the extent of mentioning global brands such as Nivea and OB). Results from the survey also showed that the European group was more likely to bring back toiletries ($\chi^2 = 8.01$, $df = 3$, $p = 0.044$).

Clothes and fashion

Clothing was not a particularly significant category in terms of allocation of 'home goods' but when this option was selected, it yielded a number of comments on quality, price, inability to locate similar items, style, range and aesthetic preferences. These were pitched in comparative terms ('there is no style like this', 'clothes in

China is much cheaper and [more] beautiful than UK style', 'I prefer the fashion of my own country'). The ability for clothing to provide emotional comfort was explicitly expressed by a student from Nigeria:

> I cannot get native clothes made here except at a very expensive price. They don't wear it here and when I miss home, I can wear them or just seeing them gives me joy.

Culturally distinctive clothing is here for private gratification. Conversely, fashion is earmarked as an unwanted sign for cultural differentiation by another international student (from South Korea):

> [I do not bring this back from home] as I am trying to suit the way that European people wear cloth

The reference in this case is one of exclusion, of leaving behind parts of one's culture in a deliberate effort to conform and blend in with the general UK student population.

Patterns of behaviour

The survey did not bring out particular patterns of change of behaviour but, as previously mentioned, most of the respondents had resided in the UK for a relatively short period of time. If comments were made it was generally about food, either to report stopping bringing in individual food items after locating them in local stores, or conversely identifying a lack of specific products in the UK. However, a hint that patterns of motivation for bringing in goods could be fairly complex transpires from the following comment made by an individual who had been residing in the UK for a longer period of time (over 5 years):

> It depends on the season and ... how I feel. Because when I first came over I did not bring much stuff and then after 6 months I just brought a lot of stuff, and by stuff I mean tobacco and food mainly ... and two years ago, three years ago I got a big carton sent by my friends. But I prepared it myself and had it shipped when I am here ... But I don't know ... I tend to bring something pretty much all the time, if I can, if I have enough space ... because sometimes I don't feel it's worth to pay extra money.. just to bring something that somehow you can find over here as well ...

Conclusion

Throughout this paper we have highlighted the ability of personal goods to provide a hiatus between home and host cultures, in particular those with a connection with the senses and perception and projection of self and mapped out conceptualisations of this relationship from different bodies of research. As previously cited, human geographers Crang et al. (2003, p. 451) see commodity as a 'lens'. The term 'collocations' could also be borrowed as a metaphor from linguistics to refer to the informative property of goods and objects in relation to their translocated human referents, informing not only on the material company that these individuals keep but also on the distilling process which has led to their election. Our research has also identified a number of potential lines of enquiry, such as the evolution of attitudes and behaviours over time and the need to disambiguate between perceptions of non-availability and need to attribute specific locating coordinates.

Notes

1. A Chi-square test is a common statistical test used to establish whether there is a significant difference between an observed set of results and the expected results (the latter based on a null hypothesis, e.g. an equal ratio or a random association between two variables), in other words to investigate whether values depart from what would be expected by chance alone. In this study we were testing results obtained from one set of questions against answers provided in another set. For instance we interrogated the data to establish whether there was a link between the geographical origin of the sample and the type of comments the respondents made. The statistical information provides the following specific data: The chi-square result χ^2 determines the significance of the pairing of the variables. The higher the χ^2 value, the more significant (i.e. the less likely due to chance) the association between the two variables is. The df value refers to the degrees of freedom which is the number of values that are free to vary after restriction has been placed on the data. The p-value is the probability of obtaining a test statistic at least as extreme as the one that was actually observed, assuming that the null hypothesis is true (according to which there is no relationship between the two measured phenomena) The lower the p-value, the less likely the result is if the null hypothesis is true, and consequently the more 'significant' the result is (i.e. the result is not likely to be due to chance). A null hypothesis is rejected if the p-value is less than a chosen threshold, most commonly 0.05 (i.e. 5% probability of the results being due to chance alone). As an example, in the first instance in the manuscript, we used this test to look for a non-random association between whether or not people brought food from home and their opinion as to whether they would be able to find any proper equivalent in this country. The test was highly significant ($\chi^2 = 11.803$, degrees of freedom = 1, probability = 0.001).
2. Sandwich in Spanish.

References

Ahuvia, A.C. (2005). Beyond the extended self: Loved objects and consumers' identity narratives. *Journal of Consumer Research, 32*(1), 171–184.

Askegaard, S., & Madsen, T.K. (1998). The local and the global: Exploring traits of homogeneity and heterogeneity in European food cultures. *International Business Review, 7*, 549–568.

Baudrillard, J. (1981). *Simulacres et Simulation* [Simulacra and Simulation]. Paris: Editions Galilée.

Belk, R.W. (1990). The role of possessions in constructing and maintaining a sense of past. *Advances in Consumer Research, 17*, 669–676.

Beverland, M., & Farrelly, F. (2010). The quest for authenticity in consumption: Consumers' purposive choice of authentic cues to shape experienced outcomes. *Journal of Consumer Research, 36*(5), 838–856.

Bourdieu, P. (1977). *Outline of a theory of practice*. Cambridge: Cambridge University Press.

Brown, L. (2009). The role of food in the adjustment journey of international students. In A. Lindgreen & M.K. Hingley (Eds.), *The new cultures of food: Marketing opportunities from ethnic, religious and cultural diversity* (pp. 37–56). Farnham: Gower Publishing.

Carrier, J. (1990). Reconciling commodities and personal relations in industrial society. *Theory and Society, 19*, 579–598.

Carroll, B., & Ahuvia, A. (2006). Some antecedents and outcomes of brand love. *Marketing Letters, 17*(2), 79–89.

Chandler, D. (2002). *Semiotics: The basics* (2nd ed). Abingdon: Routledge.

Conradson, D., & McKay, D. (2007). Translocal subjectivity: Mobility, connection and emotion. *Mobilities, 2*(2), 167–174.

Crang, P., Dwyer, C., & Jackson, P. (2003). Transnationalism and the spaces of commodity culture. *Progress in Human Geography, 27*(4), 438–456.

Cushman, P. (1990). Why the self is empty: Towards a historically situated psychology. *American Psychologist, 45*(5), 599–611 [cited by Ahuvia 2005].

Davies, A., & Fitchett, M.A. (2002). Interpretivist and positivist insights into museum consumption: An empirical enquiry into paradigm compatibility. *European Advances in Consumer Research, 5*, 234–239.

Davies, A., & Fitchett, J.A. (2004). 'Crossing culture': A multi-method enquiry into consumer behaviour and the experience of cultural transition. *Journal of Consumer Behaviour, 3*(4), 315–330.

De Mooij, M. (2010). *Consumer behaviour and culture: Consequences for global marketing and advertising* (2nd ed). London: Sage.

Epp, A., & Price, L. (2010). The storied life of singularized objects: Forces of agency and network transformation. *Journal of Consumer Research, 36*(5), 820–837.

Grayson, K., & Shulman, D. (2000). Indexicality and the verification function of irreplaceable possessions: A semiotic analysis. *Journal of Consumer Research, 27*, 17–30.

Holbrook, M.B., & Schindler, R.M. (2003). Nostalgia for early experiences as a determinant of consumer preferences. *Psychology & Marketing, 20*(4), 275–302.

Holliday, A. (2010). Complexity in cultural identity. *Language and Intercultural Communication, 10*(2), 165–177.

Kessous, A., & Roux, E. (2008). A semiotic analysis of nostalgia as a connection to the past. *Qualitative Market Research, 11*(2), 192–212.

Monceri, F. (2009). The transculturing self II: Constructing identity through identification. *Language and Intercultural Communication, 9*(1), 45–53.

Rojas Gaviria, P., & Bluemelhuber, C. (2010). Consumers' transformations in a liquid society: Introducing the concepts of autobiographical-concern and desire-assemblage. *Journal of Consumer Behaviour, 9*(2), 126–138.

Schembri, S., Merrilees, B., & Kristiansen, S. (2010). Brand consumption and narrative of the self. *Psychology & Marketing, 27*(6), 623–638.

Tolia-Kelly, D. (2004). Locating processes of identification: Studying the precipitates of re-memory through artefacts in the British Asian home. *Transactions of the Institute of British Geographers, 29*, 314–329.

Wang, Y.K., & Datta, P. (2010). Investigating technology commitment in instant messaging application users. *Journal of Organisational and End-user Computing, 22*(4), 7–94.

Language and the negotiation of identity and sense of belonging: a study of literary representations of Indians in England

Meenakshi Sharma

Department of Communications, Indian Institute of Management Ahmedabad, Ahmedabad, 380015, India

The writings of Indians in English provide a rich ground to explore the ways in which travellers and migrants from India to England relate to the realities of the place and to their place in it. Language and the literary education that characterised English education in India during colonial times play an important role in the construction of identity of such Indians. The love and idealisation of an 'imagined' England constructed from literary texts, and the encounter with reality upon travel to England, are depicted in many fictional and autobiographical accounts. Focusing on a sample of such texts from the 1950s to the 1970s, this paper looks at representations of the first-hand experience of England for those who identify themselves with Englishness on the strength of their intellectual and emotional connection with it through love for the language and literature. The study yields interesting insights that may have implications for current movements of people across the globalised world, with shared language and education as their 'intellectual' passport and a confident sense of identity and belonging with the West and its culture, based on 'familiarity' acquired through a shared language and images derived from ubiquitous media sources.

Les écrits des Indiens en anglais offrent un terrain riche pour explorer les façons dont les voyageurs et les migrants Indiens en l'Angleterre se rapportent à la réalité du lieu de même qu'à leurs perceptions sur leurs propre place dans la réalité anglaise. Langue et éducation littéraire qui caractérisaient l'enseignement en anglais dans l'Inde à l'époque coloniale jouent un rôle important dans la construction de l'identité de ces Indiens. L'amour et l'idéalisation d'une «imaginaire» Angleterre construite à partir de textes littéraires, et la rencontre avec la réalité sur Voyage en Angleterre, sont représentés dans de nombreux récits fictifs et autobiographiques. En se concentrant sur un échantillon de ces textes pour la période 1950–1970, ce document porte sur les représentations du vécu des Indiens en Angleterre, sur la force de leur lien intellectuel et affectif et sur l'amour pour la langue et la littérature. L'étude donne un aperçu intéressant qui peut avoir des répercussions sur les mouvements actuels de personnes à travers le monde globalisé, avec un langage commun, une éducation commune comme 'passeport intellectuel', avec un certain sens d'une identité commune, d'une appartenance au monde Occidental et a sa culture, sur la base d'une 'familiarité' acquise à travers une langue commune de même qu'à travers des médias ubiquistes.

Since the break-up of the British Empire, the world has been witnessing movements of formerly colonised peoples to the West, for tourism, as well as for reasons driven by economic pragmatism and the demands of global capitalism. These movements have necessarily involved negotiation and renegotiation of identities and forging relationships with people, places and cultures. Language plays an important role in these movements through the emotional connection created by the ties of the mind as well as through more practical considerations such as employment opportunities. A World Bank study reports that 'over half of international migration takes place between countries with a common language; the lion's share of such migration is between English-speaking countries' (Ozden & Schiff, 2007, p. 42). The reason for a common language being an important factor in migration is related to the particularly significant role it plays

> in the process of individual and societal integration . . . languages and accents can act as symbols of belonging or foreignness and give rise to differentiation and dis-crimination . . . [with] a good knowledge of the national language [being] central to educational success [and] . . . occupational opportunity. (Esser, 2006, p. i)

However, in distinction to travellers and immigrants from settler colonies to the former imperial centres, those from colonies such as India face a unique situation – although they share the language and feel a strong sense of identification with England, the racial difference disallows a simple equation of shared language with acceptance and easy integration.

Although India gained independence in 1947, the legacy of English education left behind by the British raj continued to have its impact on the ideas and identity formation of English-educated Indians. The writings of Indians in English from colonial times reveal the recurrent representation of Indian attitudes to English language and literature, British rule, English society, culture, and people. These attitudes are based on the indirect but strong and close relationship of English-educated Indians with England and English culture through the English language. The language provided Indians with access to the ideas of the West as well as served as a medium for expression of their distinct perspective for other Indians across the linguistic divides of the multilingual nation, as well as for wider audiences. The recent colonial past, the internalisation of idealised images derived from English literature, and the consequent identification with Englishness based on such familiarity and affection combine with a sense of nationalism and pride, to create complex and ambivalent responses to England and English culture. Fictional and autobiographi-cal narratives by Indians in English provide a rich ground to study the complex attitudes of Indians to England, its people and culture that range from caustic and satirical, to admiring and idealising.

I focus here on Indian accounts in English of travel and first-hand experience of England and examine the ways in which English-educated Indians travelling or migrating to England related to the realities of the place and to their place in it. Carrying the baggage of literature-derived strong feelings of familiarity, affection, admiration, and even identification with English culture, they expect to be completely at home in England. The painful clash of text-derived images of an 'imagined' England with first-hand encounter with reality is brought out in many narrative accounts by Indians. I use a sample of Indian autobiographical and fictional accounts in English spanning the 1950s to the 1970s to illustrate the treatment of the complex relationship of language and literature with identity and belonging for the Indian traveller and migrant to England of the first quarter century after Independence. Among other works, I consider the following texts at some length: Anita Desai's *Bye Bye Blackbird* (1971), Dilip Hiro's *A Triangular View* (1969), Nirad Chaudhuri's *A Passage to England* (1959) and S.K. Ghosh's *My English Journey* (1961).

I conclude the textual analysis of the role of English education in creating idealised mental images of England and English culture and in the construction of identifications with it, by proposing that the changes in the approach to English language and education in contemporary times have changed this role. Although the hold of English education has increased in the over six decades following Indian independence, its formative role on identity and on attitudes of idealisation of the culture it represents has diminished. Although ubiquitous images from numerous sources make the West familiar and known, they may not carry the intensity that literary sources had in the almost complete absence of any other kind of input about the culture and the place. Given the pace of change in terms of global reach of media sources and more frequent travel and interaction between people across the globe, the pivotal role of language and literary education in the process of identity formation through slow and deep acculturation, as attested by the texts under consideration, may not be as clear and straightforward today.

The exposure to, and subsequent internalisation of, English literary images was an offshoot of the introduction of a chiefly literary English education in colonial times. These images were not tempered with first-hand experience with England or even with direct contact with the British in India. The very small British population in India – fed by insecurities and sense of superiority – lived its life quite cut off from the mainstream of Indian life. Moreover, English-educated Indians usually make a distinction between the English 'at home' and Anglo-Indian society and culture. For Indians, the close 'contact' with 'real' England and Englishness made possible through English education – chiefly through literary and historical texts – meant that they actually felt a sense of superiority in identifying with 'true' Englishness.

The stress on a chiefly literary English education in colonial India was no accident, but a strategic move by the British for creating willing subjectification through admiration of the rulers' culture, as well as for administrative ease. The argument is well captured in Charles Trevelyan's words:

> The spirit of English literature...cannot but be favourable to the English connection. Familiarly acquainted with us by means of our literature, the Indian youth almost cease to regard us as foreigners. They speak of our great men with the same enthusiasm as we do. Educated in the same way, interested in the same objects, engaged in the same pursuits with ourselves, they become more English than Hindus....What is it that makes us what we are, except living and conversing with English people, and imbibing English thoughts and habits of mind? They do so too: they daily converse with the best and wisest Englishmen through the medium of their works; and form, perhaps, a higher idea of our nation than if their intercourse with it were of a more personal kind. (1838, pp. 189–190)

Gauri Viswanathan has shown how English literature was used to resolve the tension between the British stance on increasing involvement in Indian education on the one hand, and the position on non-interference in religion on the other. This move not only served practical imperatives but also the deeper ones of creating willing subjectification through 'alteration in their feelings and notions' and admiration for the ideals of the ruling race (1987, pp. 12–13). English education in colonial India became, in Ranajit Guha's words, 'a hegemonic instrument wielded in order to persuade the subject population about the desirability of its own subjection' (1988, p. 24). The success of these strategies is evident in the generations of Anglicised Indians who felt the strongest ties of the mind to England and Englishness. The 'imperishable empire of our arts and our morals, our literature and our laws' (Bennett, 1962, p. 75) envisioned by Macaulay in 1833, was thus created in the minds and hearts of the new, small but influential Indian elite of the English-educated class, and in this way, outlived the political life of the Empire.

Indian responses and attitudes to England, English literature, and culture are of great significance, pointing to the complex ways in which identity and subjectivity are negotiated within the colonial and post-colonial situation despite the inevitable co-option into the discourse of Western modernity. In the range of responses created by the ambivalence of the colonised subject to the culture of the ruling race, admiration and idealisation are situated at one end, just as the anti-colonial, tactical, and opportunistic responses that were used to ultimately erode British authority are at the other. I have looked elsewhere, at some length, at the two ends of the continuum of responses of the English-educated Indians in colonial and post-independence times (Sharma, 2003). While some internalised their (literary) exposure to Englishness and came to idealise it and to identify with it, others used it to strengthen their understanding of Western ideas and concepts and harnessed these towards the cause of nationalism. A middle ground was also visible in maintaining a distinction between the practical/external/social and spiritual/internal/domestic spheres of life (Chatterjee, 1993, p. 6). Looking at the representations of this class in Indian-English literary texts, one finds that the anglicised Indians of colonial times are often represented as caught between the opposing currents of Indian tradition and nationalist aspirations on the one hand, and admiration for English literature, language, culture, and western scientific progress on the other. Sometimes they are caricatured as misfits – ridiculous and alienated from Indian reality – and the aping of English manners and superficial adoption of Englishness is represented as the pathetic but inevitable outcome of colonial subjection. In G.V. Desani's *All About Mr. Hatterr* (1948), the character of Banerrji is used to ridicule the 'bookish' style of Anglophiles whose adulation for England is solely based on literary texts. At other times, specially in autobiographical accounts, the dilemma and ambivalences inherent in the position are more sympathetically presented.

Acquisition and consequent appropriation of language also have implications for agency and self-representation. I have, elsewhere, dealt with how educated Indians, despite their necessary involvement in the colonial process and the unavoidable transformations in their social and ideological constructions, employed their literary and autobiographical writings in the English language to resist their typification as passive objects of Orientalist discourses through their own representations of England and the English. Much Indian writing in English from the earliest times has been concerned, directly or indirectly, with refuting such essentialised and stereotypical representations of India and much of that writing has turned the gaze back upon England and the English – scrutinising, assessing, judging these from the Indian viewpoint, often in clear opposition to the English self-image (Sharma, 2003). While acknowledging the subversive potential of writing in the language of the former rulers and even more so in representing their nation and culture, I wish to focus here on a specific issue – the representations of the experience of English-educated Indians in England.

During colonial times, Indian visitors to England had often travelled under the patronage of powerful and wealthy English men or women, which generally led to positive representations of their English experiences in autobiographical accounts. Fictional accounts, however, often represented more critical attitudes to English culture. In the three decades following independence, both fictional and autobiographical accounts take a more critical view to England and Englishness and often employ a self-conscious reflectiveness in presenting attitudes and responses. With increase in number of travellers and immigrants in the post-independence period, especially in the 1960s and 1970s, many accounts deal with the direct experience of England and English culture and its clash with the mental baggage of literary images. For the English-educated Indians whose internalisation of English culture through literary texts defined their sense of identity, this encounter is often shown to result in bafflement and pain of coping with a sense of 'nowhereness'. Although their literature-derived images lead to recognition and familiarity with the land and culture and thus a corroboration of their identity as English, this experience is limited to their role as observers of the scene. On attempting to participate in English life, they are often met with rejection and an unsettling of their identity. Other recurring themes are the distinction between the English in India and in England, and the evaluation and analysis of English culture in comparison with Indian traditions as well as with the typical laudatory self-representations in English literature. That these themes are visible in narratives well into the post-independence period testifies to the lasting legacy of the introduction of English literary education in India.

Fiction

The hold of literary images of England on the minds of English-educated Indians is attested by their recurrent use in not only visualising England from afar but also in relating to the actual experience of the place. Rama in Raja Rao's *The Serpent and the Rope* (1960) describes England at the time of the Coronation as 'far from the world of Jane Austen or Thackeray, or even from the world of Virginia Woolf' (p. 200). In Victor Anant's novel *Revolving man* (1959) one of the characters coolly steps on the escalator on his first day in England, and credits this ease to reading: 'one reads about these things so much they become familiar even before you see them' (p. 212). The escalator may be taken as standing for England itself which becomes known and familiar from literary texts to many Indians.

The ambivalence of post-independence educated Indians is often shown through the self-conscious exploration of the question of language and education as constitutive of identity. For example, in Anita Desai's *Bye Bye Blackbird* (1971), Dev wonders how

> so many people in his country, of so many generations and so many social and economic classes, had been brought up on a language and literature completely alien to them, been fed it like a sweet in infancy, like a drug in youth, so that, before they realized it, they were addicts of it, their bodies were composed called . . . 'Macaulay's bastards.' This was his label too. (p. 122)

The depiction of such Anglophile characters is sometimes sympathetic and at other times done in a mocking and satirical manner. A common pattern is the representation of the clash between identification at the emotional and intellectual levels and at the level of lived experience, in a place that is found to be at the same time familiar and alien. While the English-educated characters identify with Englishness yet, this one-sided relationship of affection, admiration, and idealisation is shown to not insulate them from being shunned, resented, and regarded as aliens in England. In Dilip Hiro's *A Triangular View* (1969), the protagonist arrives in England idealising it as 'my Mecca, my England' (p. 9) and inhales deep 'for it was European air – the best' (p. 10) but after facing racist sneers his sense of identification is badly shaken and he does not 'invoke the names of Johnson and Boswell again, or of Dryden and Pope' (p. 16).

In Desai's *Bye Bye Blackbird*, this theme is worked out in great detail. When Sarah shows the newly arrived Dev the sights of London, he tells her, 'You don't have to tell me. . . . I have always known them. . . . Ever since I could read' (p. 64). He recognises the 'originals' of what he had encountered in books, and finds that 'he had known them all, he had met them before, in the pages of Dickens and Lamb, Addison and Boswell, Dryden and Jerome K. Jerome' (p. 10). Although his life so far had not even the remotest resemblance to the world of the English pub he enters, he finds it 'known, familiar, easy to touch, enjoy and accept because he was so well prepare to enter it – so well prepared by fifteen years of reading, the [English] books that had been his meat and drink' (p. 11). While in London he imagines he can almost see Dr Johnson and Dryden and Boswell walking on the same streets, and Shakespearean characters flitting about. Walking about the countryside he encounters

> the England her poets had celebrated so well that he, a foreigner, found every little wildflower, every mood and aspect of it familiar. It was something he was visiting for the first time in his life, yet he had known it all along – in his reading, in his daydreams – and now he found his dreams had been an exact, a detailed, a brilliant and mirrorlike reflection of reality. English literature! English poetry! He wanted to shout . . . (p. 170)

His sense of identity formed by such internalisation of literary images, he dreams of settling into his own home in the English countryside, like the 'blissful English authors, painters, philosophers' who lived 'in a lonely tower, an old wind-mill, a Cornish cottage' (p. 155).

However, compared to the treatment of such figures in autobiographical accounts, this fictional character is depicted as acutely conscious of his predicament. He is shown to realise that the literary diet on which he has been fed is like a 'drug' and the reality he is now encountering, a 'vision', and that this combination of 'copy and original' holds him in 'a double net', creating acute ambivalence: '[H]e asked himself if this net did not cut into his flesh, maiming him, or whether enslavement were not sweet, heady, rewarding, more fantastic than abhorrent, more true than untrue' (p. 122).

As in many fictional narratives, the happy sense of recognition and affection is limited to the role of observer and is marred by the response of English people. Dev is called 'Wog' by a schoolboy on the street, while an Englishwoman walking her dog in the park grumbles, 'littered with Asians! Must . . . move out of Clapham. It is impossible now' (p. 16). When he hears a word in the tube or notices an expression on an English face . . . he feels he can never bear to be the unwanted immigrant . . . he is perfectly aware of the schizophrenia that is infecting him like the disease to which all Indians abroad, he declares, are prone. (p. 86)

He realises that notwithstanding the rapture of encountering the real version of his literary images, and his love for England and sense of belonging, his sense of identity as an Englishman is meaningless to the English themselves:

That's the whole damn snag . . . you rush out, shouting 'Look, this is what Milton wrote about! Look, here's the Tennyson's poem in real life! Isn't it fine? Isn't it splendid?' and out comes a man with red hair, flings his duster in your face and says 'It's not for you, buster. You ain't on time. Out you get.' Phoo!' . . . Everything tells you you're an outsider and not entitled to the country just because you happen to have read and enjoyed its literature or because you belong to something called the Commonwealth. (pp. 161–162)

Adit – another character in the novel – re-emphasises the role of English education in shaping the self-perception and identity of the immigrant – he claims that he has every right to enjoy English things and life in England

because of my education, my tastes, my interest in them. No Englishman can deny them to me. . . . I'm different. I love them. I love England. I admire England. I can appreciate her history and her poetry as much as any Englishman. I feel a thrill about Nelson's battles, about Waterloo, about Churchill. (p. 164)

His position is that the educated immigrant, who admires and loves England, deserves and finds acceptance. However, he too is eventually shaken out of his comfortable sense of belonging by the insults and the racist graffiti in the London tube and comes to feel like the Indians he had despised – the 'eternal immigrants who can never accept their new home' (p. 181). He had

put down their diffidence and their failure to lack of preparation by education . . . but now his own education, his 'feel' for British history and poetry, fell away from him like a coat that had been secretly undermined by moths so that . . . [it] crumbles quietly to dust upon the wearer's shoulders. (p. 182)

The English-educated Indian's sense of identity, shaped by years of slow internalisation of literary images, is thus shown to be not strong enough to survive the encounter with reality nor is the affection for the land and culture shown to be reciprocated in the smallest measure.

Autobiographical accounts

Turning to autobiographical accounts, we find a similar recurrence of literary images brought to the mind on first-hand encounter with England. Kumara P. Menon, exploring the English countryside with friends during vacations, records his pleasure in riding and walking 'on the moors of Devon, full of memories of a favourite book of mine, *Lorna Doone*' (Menon, 1965, p. 60). Nirad Chaudhuri's *A passage to England* (1959) and S.K. Ghosh's *My English Journey* (1961) are replete with such instances of 'recognition' of scenes internalised through a literary diet.

However, unlike the self-conscious ambivalence of fictional characters, auto-biographical accounts are generally marked by a common tone of self-congratula-tion, proclaiming the author's Anglicisation of spirit. The strong sense of identification with Englishness is shown as leading naturally to confidence and ease in relating to first-hand experience of England. These subjective accounts largely focus on experiences that confirm this belief through laudatory self-representation where, unlike representations of Anglicised characters in fictional accounts, the identification with Englishness is generally shown to be unproble-matic. Only occasionally does one encounter the kind of experience shared by R. Parthasarthy of his familiarity with England and the English based on literary texts being simply shaken on actual experience, where he arrived fed on English literary texts, 'certain that I would find myself more or less at home there....[but] here was an England I was unable to come to terms with. The England I had known and loved existed nowhere except in my mind. This other England I did not know even existed' (1982, p. 66). More typical are the autobiographical accounts where there is no acknowledgement of anything other than the positive experience of recognition and acceptance based on one's deep familiarity and love for Englishness and the consequent identification with the culture. In fact, in his autobiographical essay 'The three faces of an Indian', Victor Anant goes to the extent of claiming as he leaves for England, that 'I was a Briton, *even* in the colouring of my skin' and his idealisation of England: 'If independence had resulted in self-consciousness, and self-consciousness in alienation, I was sure England would make me whole again' (1960, p. 84). Nirad Chaudhuri, the Anglophile beyond compare, stresses in his *Autobiography* [first published in 1951] that his Anglicism of spirit is based completely on texts rather than on actual contact with the English in India and that his immersion in English literature attuned him 'very successfully to the spirit of the English language and English life' (Chaudhuri, 1968, p. 149). The confrontation of these images acquired from literary readings with the 'real' England is described in his *A passage to England* (1959). The world known only through readings is so real, that there is only recognition and familiarity in actually encountering it first-hand. In a letter to his family he writes that 'England has *not* become more real to me than it was' (p. 14, emphasis added) and that 'in no case was the idea of England I had gained from books contradicted by anything I saw, it was on the contrary completed' (p. 15). In fact, if there is a discrepancy, he is clear that 'my earlier, and *as I believe truer*, ideas of England...acquired from literature, history, and geography' were to be maintained (p. 4, emphasis added). His strong feelings for English poetry as 'the most wonderful thing in the world' (p. 114) lead him to invert Rupert Brooke's feeling that if he died in a distant land 'some part of that foreign soil would become for ever England', by claiming that if he [Chaudhuri] 'died in England what would become for ever England would be a little foreign flesh, and with that faith there was happiness in perishing in an English glade, with the robin and the wren twittering overhead' (p. 115). Interestingly enough, Chaudhuri was able to achieve this dream – moving to England and settling in Oxford in his seventies, and dying there at the age of 101 in 1999.

Similarly, the self-portrait of S.K. Ghosh in *My English Journey* (1961) attempts to show himself as an Englishmen at heart who experiences no sense of alienation or disorientation on arriving in England. The London of his dreams is a patchwork of literary images and even on reaching there he sees it through the lens of these images: "'I love walking in London," said Mrs. Dalloway. So did I' (p. 133). Walking the streets of central London, he is happy to think that 'Lamb must have trudged these streets over and over again' (p. 139). His experiences only validate the ideas derived from literary texts and, as in the case of Chaudhuri, if there is a discordant note between the reality and the text-derived image, the latter is accepted rather than the former. Attesting to his feeling more English than the English, he writes of his acute distress at the 'passing of familiar things' and the gradual disappearance of a 'quintessential' England while 'no one in England' can perceive it (p. 106). His knowledge and love for 'true Englishness' make him critical 'certain social changes in England,' (p. 110) attributing them to 'the hazards of metropolitan life and a telly-snack bar culture' (p. 109). Such accounts by staunch Anglophiles provide no instance of jolts to their sense of identification with English through the behaviour of the English. In fact, the 'brown' Englishman judges and finds the English to be un-English!

The above sample of fictional and autobiographical narratives shows a range of experiences, with the dominant theme emerging from the former being that of the sense of identification being shaken on the basis of the visible alienness. With their sense of identification and belonging rejected, the Indian visitor/immigrant is shown as embittered and confused. Understandably, autobiographical accounts are more clearly sympathetic to the Anglicised Indian class to which the authors belong, and generally represent the identification with Englishness as unproblematic. Their self-portraits and experiences are constructed to present a more unshakeable sense of identification based on 'love' for the English language, deep knowledge of English literature, and through it, of the very pulse of English culture. Such accounts testify to Trevelyan's astuteness in predicting that English language and literature would allow Indians to imbibe English thoughts and habits of mind through conversing with the best and wisest Englishmen and lead them to form an idealised image of Englishness (1838, pp. 189–190). However, Trevelyan could probably not have anticipated the kind of dislocations that would result from the creation of these 'brown Englishmen' and from the encounter of their idealised images with the real place and people and culture.

Postcolonial critics have pointed to the curious position of the mimicking native who, by their in-between status, poses a challenge and threat to colonial authority. As Homi Bhabha points out, when Macaulay had conceived of the educated Indian as a 'class of interpreters between us and the millions whom we govern – a class of persons Indian in blood and colour, but English in tastes, in opinions, in morals and in intellect' it was 'a mimic man' (1984, p. 128) he was hoping to create. However, this hybrid product troubles the necessary basis of colonialism – the clear demarcation between the coloniser and the colonised – through the claim of knowing, admiring, and even identifying with 'true' Englishness. In Elleke Boehmer's words, 'mimickers reflected back to the colonizer a distorted image of his world . . . through ventriloquizing the colonizer's voice, through identifying themselves in the vocabulary of their oppression, they also mixed up and upturned dominant meanings' (1995, pp. 172–173). The discomfort of the English in England to such visitors/settlers may reflect this troubling aspect of mimicking. For the visitors/settlers themselves, the experience often exposed the limits of the intellectual and emotional bond in ensuring assimilation in the face of prejudice and ethnocentrism combined with strong economic and social forces.

The contemporary context

The literary representations focused on above give a human face to the encounter of the 'real' and 'imagined' England and provide a historical perspective on an important phenomenon of movement of people from the formerly colonised world to the centre as visitors and immigrants. Insights from these texts may have implications for current movements of people across the globalised world, with shared language and education as their 'intellectual' passport and confidence in understanding and identifying with the cultural norms. This confidence is based on knowing the language and the sense of (indirect) familiarity with the land and culture acquired through textual and other sources. They also raise pragmatic concerns of surviving and thriving in the West as travellers and migrants while dealing with the realities of racial difference and prejudice in their various manifestations. With the expansion of the globalised economy, and the prolifera-tion of information and images of the overarching Western model, the Western world begins to seem 'known' regardless of prior direct experience, to people from around the globe. Consequently, questions of identification with something known at second hand and the sense of belonging, and the impact of actual experience of visiting or settling in, are thrown up again in various forms in contemporary times. Regrettably, the world has not changed so much that questions of acceptance of others have become redundant. Moreover, the responses of unease, and even of threat, when faced with an 'other' who claims equality or displays an assumption of similarity, have probably remained as strong as ever. Stereotyping of culturally different peoples also leads to the kind of misunderstanding and rejection that the minority within a larger group face. While sections of Indians have, over a long period of time, had varying degrees of exposure to the West, the general perception in the minds of Westerners remains one of alienness, and consequently, the affection and idealisation for England/the West felt by this minority who are intellectually and culturally attuned to the West, is hardly understood or reciprocated. As a result, to a large extent, the affection, idealisation and admiration, based on a shared language and familiarity with the culture of the other, remains one-sided.

In the Indian context, the last two decades of economic liberalisation have further accelerated the demand for English education. With more and more Indians acquiring English, it would be interesting to contrast the deep impact of English education on Indians in colonial times and even for many decades after independence, with that in contemporary times. Examining the current state of English in India, one finds that the motives of learners as well as the pedagogy, and even the language itself, have undergone significant changes reflective of the changing status of the language. Indians have recognised, as have others around the world, that 'without English you are not even in the race' (Graddol, 2006, p. 122). At the same time, the 'function and place [of English] in the curriculum is no longer that of "foreign language" and this is bringing about profound changes in who is learning English, their motives for learning it and their needs as learners' (Graddol, 2006, p. 72). The growing demand for English education in India has been accompanied by stress on indigenising of both curricula and pedagogy with far-reaching implications on the impact of the education. This is not unique to India, but a trend around the world. Mark Warkschauer points to the shift to a 'communicative approach' that has shaken the strong connection between language and culture by focusing on 'functional interaction rather than on the achievement of nativelike perfection' and that this trend corresponds to the imperatives of the contemporary world in which English is shared among many groups of nonnative speakers rather than dominated by the British or Americans (Warkschauer, 2000, p. 512).

Thus, with English having acquired the position of a global lingua franca for international business, science, publishing, and computers, its older associations with literature and culture of a 'superior' race based on the use of the language as a tool for the Englishman's civilising mission across the empire, seem to have been largely displaced by more pragmatic ones of acquiring a tool/skill and as an indicator of power, prestige, and success. The current status of English is captured well by Fishman (1998/1999):

> Although English is the mother tongue of only 380 million people, it is the language of the lion's share of the world's books, academic papers, newspapers, and magazines. American radio, television, and blockbuster films export English-language pop culture worldwide. More than 80 percent of the content posted on the Internet is in English, even though an estimated 44 percent of online users speak another language in the home. Not surprisingly, both the global supply of and the demand for English instruction are exploding. (p. 26)

At the same time, although more and more people around the world are now learning English, they are doing so because of its value as an international language for communication rather than because of its cultural associations.

Moreover, the language itself has not remained static and, in the times to come, will become 'what its speakers make of it, and those speakers are increasingly going to be from developing and newly industrialized countries in Asia, Africa, the Middle East, and Latin America' (Warkschauer, 2000, p. 530). Already, the language has morphed into 'Englishes' with its adoption and adaptation/appropriation by non-native speakers around the world. This has also contributed to breaking down the strong older associations with the idea of a culturally superior 'centre'. Acquisition of the language in such a context is not likely to produce the kind of intense, intimate, and deep familiarity with a particular culture through its literary output. Such an education was designed to subtly create willing subjectification through admiration and acculturation and in this it succeeded spectacularly as attested by the attitudes of generations of Indians. The kinds of representations of love and admiration leading to strong identification with Englishness that we find in the texts above, hail to a period when, for a very small minority, and for the intended purpose of creating willing subjectificaton of the colonial Indian, an unintended offshoot was created in the psyche of those who began to define their identity as English. This, then, had implications for travel and actual encounter with England and English people.

Along with having a quite different relationship with the English language, the English-educated Indian class today lives in a world that has become smaller and surrounded by hordes of images through ubiquitous media sources. Compared to earlier times when the written word and especially literary writings were the major source of images for the educated person, the citizens of today's globalised capitalist economy absorb a greater multitude of visual images of the West, and form notions about it. They may thus acquire not only a sense of being culturally aware but even go towards defining their own identity as 'westernised' persons who 'know' the West well, and the consequent confidence that they would have no difficulty in fitting in, and in finding acceptance in the West. Combined with a superficial homogeneity that seems to be sweeping urban spaces around the globe, today's traveller from India to the West may, consequently, carry a lower sense of wonder and awe and experience a greater sense of recognition and familiarity. However, the kind of internalisation that resulted from long immersion in the language, and through it, in the literary output that captured the external and internal landscape of the land, people, and culture, is hard to achieve through the images that are received from visual and other media in contemporary times – images that may be more colourful and multitudinous but lacking in the kind of deep and lasting impact that literary readings produced. The superficial, and even tawdry, acquaintance with the West through the internet, cinema, television, and other popular media, combined with the functional use of English for communication, and the disjunction between the English language and a particular culture, is hardly likely to result in the kind of idealisation one finds in the case of the English-educated Indians of the colonial and early post-Independence period. Thus, while there may still be identification with the west and self-definition as 'westernised' based on a common language and 'familiarity' based on second-hand images and even, in some cases, on actual contact with Westerners – yet, it is likely to be of a quite different kind and intensity in comparison to that of educated Indians whose sole source of ideas and images about England (and the generalised 'West') was literature. A deeper, longer, and slower absorption of ideas almost unknowingly from texts, during an impressionable age, and in the almost complete lack of first-hand experience of the culture led to a deep internalisation of the images and ideas and often led to an extremely strong sense of identifying oneself with Englishness. This, in turn, led to the curious experience so often encountered in Indian accounts as seen above, of immediate recognition and sense of homecoming on the one hand, and hurt and bewilderment in the face of rejection and outright racism, on the other.

The intensely emotional connection with England as 'home' and the response to visiting England as a homecoming that is reflected in many Indian accounts of the period examined above, is hardly likely to be encountered in the case of contemporary users of English. The 'brown Englishmen' of earlier times – products of a long and deep familiarity with Englishness through language and a literary education, and the English-educated Indians of today are quite different in the relationship with England and the West. It may be revelatory to study from representations of contemporary fictional and autobiographical writing how the assumptions of Indians who identify with Western-ness in contemporary times stand up to actual experience. With a new set of sources of images about the West, and a changed relationship with the English language, the quality and intensity of the love and admiration for the place and the culture is also likely to have undergone a change. Compared with the kinds of images and experience captured from the literary representations of the 1950s to the 1970s, contemporary narratives by Indian travellers may reveal a sense of identification based on less deep insight into western culture and less depth of feeling for it, and consequently a milder shock on challenges to the identification of oneself as 'English' or 'Western'.

References

Anant, V. (1959). *The revolving man*. London: MacGibbon & Kee.

Anant, V. (1960). The three faces of an Indian. In T. O'Keefe (Ed.), *Alienation* (pp. 79–92). London: MacGibbon & Kee.

Bennett, G. (Ed.). (1962). *The concept of empire, Burke to Attlee, 1774–1947*. London: Adam and Charles Black.

Bhabha, H.K. (1984). Of mimicry and man: The ambivalence of colonial discourse. *October, 28*, 125–133.

Boehmer, E. (1995). *Colonial and postcolonial literature: Migrant metaphors*. Oxford: Oxford University Press.

Chatterjee, P. (1993). *The nation and its fragments: Colonial and postcolonial histories*. Princeton, NJ: Princeton University Press.

Chaudhuri, N. (1959). *A passage to England*. London: Macmillan.

Chaudhuri, N. (1968). *The autobiography of an unknown Indian*. Berkeley: University of California Press.

Desai, A. (2006). [First published 1971]. *Bye bye blackbird*. New Delhi: Orient Paperback.

Desani, G.V. (1948). *All about Mr. Hatterr: A gesture*. London: Aldor.

Esser, H. (2006). Migration, language and integration. *AKI Research Review, 4*, 1–117.

Fishman, J.A. (1998). *Foreign Policy, 113*, 26–40.

Ghosh, S.K. (1961). *My English journey*. Calcutta: Writers Workshop.

Graddol, D. (2006). *English next*. British Council.

Guha, R. (1988). *An Indian historiography of India: A nineteenth century agenda and its implications*. Calcutta: K.P. Bagchi.

Hiro, D. (1969). *A Triangular View*. London: Dobson Books.

Menon, K.P. (1965). *Many worlds: An autobiography*. London: Oxford University Press.

Parthasarathy, R. (1982). Whoring after English gods. In G. Amirthanayagam (Ed.), *Writers in East West encounter: New cultural bearings* (pp. 64–84). London: Macmillan.

Raja, Rao. (1960). *The serpent and the rope*. London: John Murray.

Ozden, C., & Schiff, M. (Eds.). (2007). *International migration, economic development & policy*. Washington DC: World Bank Publications.

Sharma, M. (2003). *Postcolonial Indian writing in English: Between co-option and resistance*. Jaipur: Rawat.

Trevelyan, C.E. (1838). *On the education of the people of India*. London: Orme, Brown, Green and Longmans.

Viswanathan, G. (1987). The beginnings of English literary study in India. *Oxford Literary Review, 9*(1–2), 2–26.

Warkschauer, M. (2000). The changing global economy and the future of English teaching. *TESOL Quarterly, 34*(3), 511–535.

Travelling languages? Land, languaging and translation

Alison Phipps

University of Glasgow, GRAMNET, University Avenue, Glasgow G12 8QQ, UK

What does translation become if we uncouple language from culture and link language to perception and experience of the land? What would happen to translation if the culture concept was not the starting point for theorizing? In order to answer this question I examine the contributions of Eagleton, Keesing, Cronin and, most particularly, of the anthropologist Tim Ingold and his important work *The Perception of the Environment*. From this I then proceed to examine pertinent extracts of the works of two Celtic authors; Brian Friel's *Translations* and Margaret Elphinstone's *A Sparrow's Flight* in order to develop a relationally grounded view of translation. This view privileges both the land and the work of *languaging* as key aspects of translation, inhabiting positions *in the world*, rather than constructing and mediating views *of the world*. I therefore come to see translation as a mode of perception, a sensory even empathic mode, a *languaging* response to phenomena, its primary relationship, not with culture and genealogy but as positionality – *in and with the land* and to develop towards a geopoetics of the *taskscape* of the translator.

አንድን ቋንቋ ከከባቢ ባህሉ ነጥለን ከሌላ ሀገር አመለካከትና ልምድ ጋር ብናቆራኘው በትርጉሙ ላይ ምን ውጤት ይከሰታል? የንድፈ ሀሳቡ መነሻ የባህሉ አሳቤ ካልሆነ የትርጉም ሥራ ውጤቱ ምን ይሆናል? የሚሉትን ጥያቄዎች በዚህ ጥናት ለመመለስ እሞክራለሁ፡ ፡ ይህን ጥያቄ ለመመለስ የኢግልተንን፣ የኪሲንግን፣ የክሮኒንን ሥራዎችና በተለይም የአንትሮፖሎጂስቱ ቲም ኢንጎልድን የአካባቢ ግንዛቤ የተሰኘ ሥራ አመረምራለሁ፡፡ እነርሱም የበራያን ፍራይል የትርጉም ሥራዎችና የማርጋሬት ኤልፊኒስተን የስፓሮ ወፍ በራ የተሰኘ መጽሐፍ ሲሆኑ፣ ተዛምዷዊነትን መሠረት ያደረገ የትርጉም አሳቤን ለማሳደግ ጠቃሚ ናቸው፡፡ ይህ አመለካከት በዓለም ውስት የሚገኙ አተያየቶችን ከመቆጣጠርና ከማስታረቅ ይልቅ፣ የቋንቋ አጠቃቀም ተግባር እንዲሁም ሥፍራው የትርጉም ሥራ ቁልፍ ገፅታዎች ማንኛቸውን በአፅንዖት የሚያራምድና በዚህ ረገድ በዓለም ውስት ለምንኖርበት ከባቢያዊ ማዕቀፍ ቅድሚያ የሚሰት ነው፡፡ ስለሆነም ይህ ጥናት የትርጉምን ተግባር የሚመለከተው እንደ ስሜት-ግንዛቤ፣ የጥልቅ ስሜት መገለጫና የነባራዊ ክስተት ሥነ-ቃላዊ ምላሽ ሲሆን፣ የትርጉም ሥራ በዋነኛነት የሚያመለክተው ከባህልና ከሀረገ-ትውልድ ይልቅ ከሥፍራው ማዕቀፈ-ከባቢነት (positionality) እንደመሆኑ በተጨማሪው አድማዋ-ተግባር ወደ ሉላዊሥነቃልነት (geopoetics) ይጎለብታል፡፡

Dieser Artikel versucht die folgende Frage zu beantworten: Was geschieht mit einer Übersetzung, wenn Sprache und Kultur voneinander getrennt gedacht, und stattdessen Sprache mit der Wahrnehmung und Erfahrung von *Land/Erde/Boden* verbunden wird? Was würde mit einer Übersetzung passieren, wenn das kulturelle Konzept nicht der Ausgangspunkt für das Theoretisieren wäre? Um diese Frage zu beantworten, werden Beiträge von Eagleton, Keesing, Cronin und ganz besonders von Anthropologe Tim Ingold untersucht. Der Artikel geht dann dazu über eine in Beziehungen begründete, phänomenologische Sichtweise auf Übersetzung zu entwickeln. Diese Sichtweise hebt besonders *Land* und *languaging* als Schlüsselaspekte von Übersetzung hervor: das Bewohnen von Haltungen und Einstellungen in der Welt, im Gegensatz zu der Konstruktion und Vermittlung von Weltsichten. Der Artikel tritt für eine

Sichtweise auf Übersetzung als eine Art von Wahrnehmung ein, die sensorisch und gleichsam einfühlend ist und eine *languaging*-Antwort auf Phänomene darstellt, die nicht zuerst mit Kultur und Geneaologie einhergeht, sondern als Positionalität auftritt – im und mit dem *Land- der Erde* und welche entwickelt werden kann im Sinne einer Geopoetik in Bezug auf die Aufgabenlandschaft des Übersetzers.

Prologue: The Angel of the North

I think I stand outside the mainstream discourses certainly of postmodernism, which would see some of the premises I work from as very problematic, such as the proposition that bodily experience (and indeed the way the body expresses itself) is a language before language. They would say that there are no dialogues, real or internal, that are not culturally given; and I would say that that's just not true. When you dive into the sea or eat your breakfast or whatever, these are very straight forward, direct, first hand-hand experiences which are not culturally conditioned. And they're the ones that I'm interested in. (Anthony Gormley in *Third Way*, March 2005, p. 17)

Introduction

The term 'languaging' is the starting point for conceptualising the approach this paper takes to travelling languages and translation. It is a term I developed together with my colleague Mike Gonzalez (Phipps & Gonzalez, 2004). It has been used before in different contexts and at different times in history. It emerged for us out of the process of struggling to find a way of articulating the full, embodied and engaged interaction with the world that comes when we put the languages we are learning into action. We make a distinction between the effort of using languages that one is learning in the classroom contexts with the effort of being a person in that language in the social and material world of everyday interactions. 'Languagers', for us, are those people, we may even term them 'agents' or 'language activists', who engage with the world-in-action, who move in the world in a way that allows the risk of stepping out of one's habitual ways of speaking and attempt to develop different, more relational ways of interacting with the people and phenomena that one encounters in everyday life. 'Languagers' use the ways in which they perceive the world to develop new dispositions for poetic action in another language and they are engaged in developing these dispositions so that they become habitual, durable.

Beyond culture?

Recent work in anthropology and in cultural studies has cast doubt on the continued privileging of the concept of culture as a useful explanatory device or starting point for analysis. The skeptics of the culture concept have not come to their position lightly, but have laboured with it and with increasing frustration as they have used the term repeatedly and come to feel its brokenness. Culture is a concept which now struggles to bear the weight of the load we impose upon it. Terry Eagleton, in *The Idea of Culture* (2000) and in *After Theory* (2003)*,* tackles the way the culture concept has been used and, as he sees it, abused in the culture wars that have raged across the humanities in recent decades:

> Those radicals for whom high culture is *ipso facto* reactionary forget that much of it is well to the left of the World Bank [...] What matters is not the works themselves but the way they are collectively construed, ways which the works could hardly have anticipated [...] It is not Shakespeare who is worthless, just some of the social uses to which his work has been put. (Eagleton, 2000, p. 52)

Culture is a problematic term. It is ideology ridden. It starts culture wars, it atomises and it shifts politics from human suffering to questions of cultural identity. The logical end of the argument reached by Eagleton is that the term needs to be put firmly in its place, for it has become too overweening, too woolly, too imprecise. In Eagleton's view culture is no longer a helpful discursive construct. It creates more problems than it solves. In Gillian Rose's (1992) terms, it serves the diremption between law and ethics, seeking to 'mend' what she terms 'the broken middle' with identity politics or vague notions of 'community'.

In anthropology, the field that was founded on ideas of cultural difference, there have been similar rumblings of discontent with the term. Roger Keesing, for instance, is troubled by both the concept of culture and its attendant translation baggage:

> It has been anthropology's role to provide the exotic alternative culturally constructed universes that are the counters to Western ones [...] 'if Radical Alterity did not exist, it would be anthropology's task to create it'. We have been professional dealers in exotica, going to romantic and distant places and coming back to recount all manner of strange beliefs and practices as if they were unremarkable. We have done our job well, it would seem, in conveying to our colleagues in other disciplines the idea of extreme cultural differences. We have succeeded in introducing our once-peculiar concept of 'culture' into popular thought and lay usage; the once jarring idea that moving from one culture to another entails radical translation is now commonplace. (Keesing, 1994, p. 3)

Ingold, coming at the problems from the anthropology of perception and cognition also struggles with the term.

> It could be said, I suppose, that through the deployment of the concept of culture anthropology has created the problem of translation rather than solved it. Having divided the world, through an operation of inversion, we are now left with the pieces that have to be connected together again through translation. Would it not be preferable to move in the opposite direction, to recover the foundational continuity, and from that basis to challenge the hegemony of an alienating discourse? If so, then the concept of culture, as a key term of that discourse, will have to go. (Ingold, 1993, p. 230)

In order to rethink the world as continuous, dwelt in and translatable, rather than exotically, even fetishistically divided up, *constructed* and where translation is a problem, Ingold turns to theories of perception in anthropology in order to develop

> [A] conception of the human being not as a composite entity made up of separable but complementary parts, such as body, mind and culture, but rather as a singular locus of creative growth within a continually unfolding field of relationships. (Ingold, 2000, pp. 4–5)

His contribution is, I believe, of some considerable importance to our understanding of translation.

In his attempts to wrestle with the legacies of the mind:body dualisms in the anthropology of perception and cognition Ingold demonstrates the powerful hold of conceptions of the mind as a discrete powerful computer processing sensory data from the world out there. Against this, grounded in a considerable literature that moves from viewing the mind as somehow stopping at the skin (Ingold, 2000, p. 3), this emergent proposition allows for us to learn to see the person as the organism, not just as a culturally constructed subject. The theoretical mainstream, in anthropology and elsewhere, persists, Ingold argues, in seeing the biological life of the organism as separate from the cultural life of the mind in society. Culture is repeatedly imposed – as verb or noun or even adjective – upon the environment rather than seeing this relationship as reciprocal and as not ending at the ends of the body.

In order to move outside of the captivities of models of culture Ingold proposes a notion of relational thinking and in his later work he links this idea to our definition of language (Ingold, 2011, pp. 174, 250).

> I had assumed that my task was not to challenge accepted biological wisdom but to reconcile it with what contemporary anthropology has to teach us about the constitution of human beings as persons. This is that the identities and characteristics of persons are not bestowed upon them in advance of their involvement with others but are condensations of histories of growth and maturation within fields of social relationships. Thus every person emerges as a locus of development within such a field, which in turn is carried forward and transformed by their actions. (Ingold, 2000, p. 3)

How does this relational, ecological view of relations among humans as encompassing more than just the socio-cultural domains traditionally ascribed to them, impact on our understanding of translation? Translation, under Ingold's theory of perception, becomes a sensory mode of perception. It moves from being a genealogical concept to being a relational concept. Echoing Deleuze and Guattari (1988) he too has 'tired of trees' – those symbols of genealogical kinship – and prefers the rhizome – the dense tangled cluster of interlaced threads or filaments any point in which can be connected to any other (Ingold, 2000, p. 140). This is the earthy model Ireland's foremost translation scholar and cultural critic Michael Cronin privileges in his article 'Thou shalt be one with the birds': Translation, connexity and the New Global Order (Cronin, 2002a, p. 94) where he draws an analogy between the work of the earth worms and the work of translators. 'Moving from the natural ecosystem to the cultural ecosystem,' he says 'it is time cultural critics turned their eyes to what lies beneath the ground of cultures, the soil which nourishes their continued vitality.'

If we shift from only examining translation culturally, as constructing cultures (Bassnett & Lefevere, 1998); as 'gendered' as 'postcolonial' as 'technocratic' and as implicated in all manner of problematic, ethically dubious or politically desirable cultural possibilities, to also examining translation as a mode of sensory relationship, then we are enabled to move beyond cultural and genealogical 'tree-like' theorizing to relational possibilities which are, yes, intercultural, but which, again to use Ingold's terms, are also *interagentic*. In other words, we are brought, in our thinking about translation, into relationships with the *exosomatic* phenomenological dimensions of our human existence (Cronin, 2002b). We come to notice the agency asserted by *techne*, by other objects, the air, the soil, the rise and fall of the land, the city – as the place of cultural concentration and growing (in Europe at least) around the housing of those 'translated' saints' bones, around what are now material objects, not human agents.

Cronin maintains that: 'the technical environment of human beings is consubstantial with our ability as speaking subjects to conceive of ourselves as human beings or beings of a particular kind of biosphere' (Cronin, 2002b, p. 2). He sees this as having profound implications for the work of translation which means that:

> [...] concentration on translation objects alone, whether they be texts or tools, will not tell us a great deal about the role of translation [...] In a properly integrated approach to translation, it is necessary to consider not only the general symbolic system (human language), the specific code (the language(s) translated), the physical support (stone, papyrus, CD-ROM), the means of transmission (manuscript, printing, digital communication) but also how translations are carried through societies over time by particular groups. (Cronin, 2002b, p. 3)

What Ingold, coming at translation from anthropology, and Cronin, from the heart of translation studies both argue, then, is that by seeing culture as somehow discrete and separate from ecological relations, from relations with the non-human world and from our interpretation and use of material life, we have created the problem of translation, or, perhaps to be more precise we have created translation to be a problem. The long list of negative metaphors and characterizations of translators as tricksters, fraudsters and women certainly points to this, as does the agonizing over invisibility by some translation scholars (Venuti, 1995).

If translation, far from being a troubling place for transmitting or constructing culture across a gaping chasm, becomes a sensory, what I together with Mike Gonzalez (Phipps & Gonzalez, 2004) would term a *languaging* response to the phenomena that present themselves in the world, then the category of translation as a cultural category, predicated upon mind:body dualisms, breaks open. Far from only being linked culturally or biologically to radical Others, whose languages we have to master and whose words and representations of life we have to translate, translation becomes a form of *interagentic* listening and speaking, of object – relations, sensory perception, the touching of meaning and a synaesthesia of communication. As Heaney puts it; *The Ash tree is cold to look at*. Or in Rilke's words from his final *Sonnett an Orpheus*; 'Zu der stillen Erde sag ich rinne, zu dem raschen Wasser sprich ich bin' [To the quiet earth say I'm running, to the rushing water say I am].

Such a move is not an easy one to make given the lexical fixation of theorizing in the arts, humanities and social sciences over the last thirty years. Representation has been our bread and butter, without the politics of identity we are left with few familiar causes, without radical cultural difference anthropology could be in some trouble. We have been working hard, as Rose says – if I am understanding her at all correctly – to mend the middle, to take the spirits out of bodies, the land out of culture, the material life out of technology, to make a problem or a virtue out of translation: all is fixed as different, diverse, and power is only dangerous.

> *We are both equally enraged and invested*, and to fix our relation in domination or dependence is unstable and reversible, to fix it as 'the world' is to attempt to avoid these reversals. All dualistic relations to 'the other', to 'the world' are attempts to quieten and

deny the broken middle, the third term which arises out of misrecognition of desire, of work, of my and your self-relation mediated by the self-relation of the other. (Rose, 1996, p. 75)

James Clifford (1997) describes translation for anthropologists as an activity that is not centred and rooted but is part of the dynamics of 'being between'. In other words it is about being the broken middle, about feeling the full, messy, liminal flow of meaning through living, translating, sensing human beings.

And this is where, for me, it gets exciting. At the crossroads of linguistic and cultural translation and the intersections with the biosphere we find translation – particularly in the recent work of Michael Cronin and Tim Ingold – as a sensory activity, that orders language alongside other sensory experiences and that touches, tastes, sees and smells meaning, as well as speaking it: Here we find a view of translation that develops, phenomenologically, out of living experiences of direct perception – that is, out of the full synaesthesia of 'being present' to the throbbing disorienting dimensions of a new, strange environment. Baudelaire returns: 'La Nature est un temple oú de vivants piliers / Laissent parfois sortir de confuse paroles; / L'homme y passé à travers de forêts de symboles / Qui l'observerent avec des regards familiars' (Correspondances). [Nature is a temple where living pillars / occasionally let slip confused words / Man [sic] passes through a forest of symbols there / which observe him with familiar glances]. The blood and bone of the translator extending themselves into language and earth, air, fire, water and grasping after meaning. 'Il est de parfums frais comme des chairs d'enfants, / doux comme les hautbois, verts comme les prairies / – Et d'autres, corrompus, riches et triomphants, / Ayant l'expansion des choses infinies, / Comme l'arbre, le musc, le benjoin et l'encens / Qui chantent les transports de L'esprit et des sens.' (Ibid.) [There are scents as fresh as a child's skin / soft as the oboe, green as the meadows / and others, corrupted, rich and triumphant / possessing the expansiveness of infinite things / like trees, musk, the rising of incense and benzion/which sing out the delight of spirit and sense].

This is where Gormley's description of the process of sculpture begins, that we encounter at the outset; 'When you dive into the sea or eat your breakfast or whatever, these are very straight forward, direct, first hand-hand experiences which are not cultural conditioned. And they're the ones that I'm interested in' (Gormley, 2005, p. 17).

And these are the very elements out of which Brian Friel, Ireland's foremost living playwright, creates a relationship between two people that tentatively grasps after meaning in translation:

Yolland: Yes-yes? Go-on – say anything at all – I love the sound of your speech
Marie:-et es in castris quae –quae –quae sunt in agro – (the futility of it) – O my God
Yolland smiles, he moves towards her. Now for her English words.
George – water.
Yolland: 'Water'? Water! Oh yes – water – water very good – water – good – good.
Marie: Fire.
Yolland: Fire – indeed – wonderful – fire, fire, fire – splendid –splendid!
Marie: Ah…ah…
Yolland: Yes? Go on.
Marie: Earth.
Yolland: 'Earth'?
Marie: Earth. Earth.
Yolland still does not understand. Marie stoops down and picks up a handful of clay.

Holding it out.
Earth.
Yolland: Earth. Of course. – earth! Earth. Earth. Good Lord, Marie, your English is perfect.
(Friel, *Translations*, pp. 63–64)

It is to Friel's *Translations* and to the work of one of Scotland's foremost contemporary novelists, Margaret Elphinstone, in her book *A Sparrow's Flight* that I now wish to turn in order to insantiate the possibilities of the sensory and relational possibilities of translation. I present these words as 'naming' phenomenon, aware of the distanciation that is inevitable when the immediate Scots-Irish-Norse context is but partially known to the audience, but as part of the deliberate methodology of this work and as a way of speaking in, of and with languages. For some this may be profoundly evocative, for others, these Norse, Viking, Gaelic remnants will be strange.

Land: From genealogy to relationship

'The names of the mountains,' said Thomas, standing up. 'They were made by shepherds like myself many centuries before the land was abused, and before the world was changed. The names were remembered in al the years of exile, and so I know them now.'
'And I am a stranger. You're willing to tell me?'
'Come here,' said Thomas.
She went over to him, and he took her by the shoulders and turned her round, so she had her back to him, facing east. 'These are the names of the mountains as they were named by my people, and have been remembered ever since, through all the generations of exile, and as I inherited them.'
'To the east,' – he pointed over her shoulder, so she could follow the direction of his arm – 'in the far distance: *High Street, Doup Crag, Red Screes,* and in front of them, *High Raise,* beyond it, *Pavey Ark,* and the two outcrops, *Harrison Stickle, Pike o' Stickle.*'
He turned her slowly southwards. '*Wetherlam, Pike o' Blisco, Swirl How, Old Man of Coniston, Grey Friar, Crinkle Crags, Bow Fell, Esk Pike, Alan's Crag, Ill Crag, Great End.*' The bulk of their own summit was in front of them now, a long plateau stretching from south to west. '*Ling Mell,*' recited Thomas, turning her to face the west, '*Middle Fell, Yowe's Barrow,* the one below it, *Seat Alan, Grey Gavel, Red Pike, Green Gavel, Scoat Fell, Pillar, Brandeth, High Crags, High Stile, Blake's Fell, Carling Knott, Mellbreak, Fleetwith Pike, Low Pike, Low Fell.*' They were turning now from west to north. '*Grass Moor, Wandope, Eel Crag, Sail, Grisedale Pike, Lord's Seat, Maiden Moor, Cat Bells.* And the line in front of those: *Robinson's Fell, Dale Head, High Spy.*'
Thomas let out a long breath, and faced her due north. '*Long Side, Carl Side, Skiddaw, Skiddaw's Little Man, Lonscale Fell, High Pike, Blencathra, Souther Fell, Clough Head, Great Dodd, Stybarrow Dodd, Raise, While Side, Helvellyn, Nethermost Pike, Dolly-waggon Pike, Fair Field, Hart Crag.* In front of them: *Blaeberry Fell, High Seat, Ullscarf.* And just below us: *Eagle Crag.*'
'Those are the names of the mountains. There are many more, which you don't see from here.'
Naomi looked at them again, turning in a slow circle of her own. 'And this one? What is the name of this one?'
'The place where you stand now,' said Thomas, smiling at her so that she was suddenly and irrelevantly aware that she loved him ' is called *Glaramara.*'
'Glaramara,' repeated Naomi. 'It should be the name of a tune.' Make it one' said Thomas
(Elphinstone, *A Sparrow's Flight* (pp. 112–113)

Ingold maintains, under his relational, sensory model, that 'Moving together along a trail, or encamped at a particular place, companions draw each other's attention, through speech or gesture, to silent features of their shared environment' (Ingold, 2000, p. 146). Eagleton suggests that 'Languages open on to the world from the inside. To be inside a language is to be pitched into the world, not to be quarantined from it' (Eagleton, 2003, p. 62).

The land evokes feelings, memories; it is like the Proustian Madeleine or Benjamin's collections of books which take him all over the world as he unpacks:

> Now I am on the last half-emptied case and it is way past midnight. Other thoughts fill me than the ones I am talking about – not thoughts but images, memories. Memories of the cities in which I found so many things: Riga, Naples, Danzig, Moscow, Florence, Basel, Paris: memories of Rosenthal's sumptuous rooms in Munich [. . .] memories of the rooms where these books have been housed, of my student's den in Munich, of my room in Bern, of the solitude of Iseltwald. (Benjamin, 1973)

Being in the land, inhabiting the land, moving through it with varied-others – leads, Ingold argues, not so much to the generation of representations to be imposed on the world as to the embodiment of *feelings of sensation.* So when Marie's first words of English uttered in love are those of water, fire and earth – the words which lead her to draw the words of the air from her lover's body in a kiss – they come not from a cultural dimension of their social being, not from the political and military and cartographical work that is the backdrop to this drama, but from the *feeling,* the touch, of the elements of life. The flesh is made word, rather than the word being made flesh.

And when Thomas stands on the hills, with his travelling companion, their names, and their careful holding as a promised land, flow from his tongue. Naomi has accompanied him for fourteen days but it is only here, on the summit of *Glaramara*, with her at his side that the naming can make any sense, that she can stand with him and empathise with the words and the land as they resonate with memory, ritual, history to come together into a flood of embodied feeling and the land can be adequately translated.

Language does not need to be passed on genealogically, it does not only equate to kinship or trees, it can be given in other ways, through eros – in Friel's example – through friendship – agape – in Elphinstone's. But it does need a position, it needs the land, material life and its imagination. In both places where translations are taught, worked out, shared, developed, we see companions on the same trail, for a time, working together on the task of translation because this is the work of relation, with each other and with the land. It is not just *cultural work.* It offers us a glimpse of the exosomatic, and of other ways of relating to place, and to words.

But it does more than this, for in both scenes our characters do the physical work with words for us. 'Glaramara', says Naomi. . . .testing the words on her tongue, feeling the dialect as odd, strange, heavy, related to this very place and time of languaging. She is not fluent, like Thomas, for her, this is not a ready connection, not yet, but she is working her way into the relations with the land and with its speakers who might take her into fluency, where fluency might mean:

> Overcoming awkwardness, halting pauses, breaks, not a simple matter of endlessly revisiting sound patterns, but of coming to recognize why and in what circumstances a thing is said, where and by whom. Fluency is the bedding of rehearsals – <u>practices</u> – into

the body and material life. It is an accumulation of stories, connection, memory, material, history, routine and ritual, work and reflection. And that is learned, developed in the context of languaging as opposed to mere language acquisition. (Phipps & Gonzalez, 2004, p. 118)

And neither Yolland nor Marie are fluent, in Friel's *Translations*. Let's listen:

Languaging: translation as embodiment of feeling

Marie: Shhh. (she holds her hand up for silence – she is trying to remember her one line of English. Now she remembers it and she delivers the line as if English were her language – easily, fluidly, conversationally.) George, in Nolfolk we besport ourselves around the maypoll.

Yolland: Good God, do you? That's where my mother comes from – Norfolk, Norwich actually. Not exactly Norwich town but a small village called Little Walsingham close beside it. But in our own village of Winfarthing we have a maypole too and every year on the first of May –

He stops abruptly, only now realizing. He stares at her. She in turn misunderstands his excitement.

Marie (to herself): Mother of God, my Aunt Mary wouldn't have taught me something dirty, would she?

Pause.

Yolland extends his hand to Marie. She turns away from him and moves slowly across the stage.

Yolland: Marie

She still moves away

Marie Chatach

She still moves away

Bun na hAbhann? *(He says the name softly, almost privately, tentatively, as if he were searching for a sound she might respond to. He tries again)* Druim Dubh?

Marie stops. She is listening. Yolland is encouraged.

Poll na gCaorach. Lis Moal.

Marie turns towards him.

Lis na nGall.

Marie: Lis na nGradh

They are now facing each other and begin moving, almost imperceptibly – towards one another

Carraig an Phoill

Yolland: Carraig na Ri, Lach n nEan

Marie: Loch an Iubhair. Machaire Buidhe.

Yolland: Mcahire Mor. Cnoc na Mona

Marie: Cnoc na nGabhar

Yolland: Mullach

Marie: Port

Yolland: Tor

Marie: Lag

She holds our her hands to Yolland. He takes them.

(Friel, *Translations*, pp. 65–66)

In Friel's *Translations* the love scene is a scene where the varied feelings of love are embodied in the speaking of names that find translation not word to word but sense to sense, phonetic touch to phonetic touch. The speaking of the names of places becomes a *languaging* response to phenomena, a way of living in translated worlds, the worlds that meet in relations and that come to make sense through these relations.

Yolland is not so much learning a language as *languaging*. He has felt the resonance of the Irish names for the land where his love resides. He is in Ireland, in Baille Beag/Bally Beg, to undo the Irish language and produce a map which replaces the Irish with English names. The work tears in to him and tears him in two, for the land speaks to him in a different tongue. His relation with this land is such that when he listens he hears Irish not English from his position within it.

And for me too, when I walk the hills of Scotland I find myself drawn into this move. The maps are strange, covered in enduring Gaelic names. They may translate or even be translated in the guidebooks and on the tourist maps, but the military maps – unlike those produced for colonized Ireland in the nineteenth century – interestingly retain the Gaelic: Buachaille Etive Mor, Buachaille Etive Beag – the Big Shepherd Etive, the little Shepherd of Etive – Carn Dearg – the red hill, Beinn Vrackie – the speckled hill. And so for Scottish walkers, who learn to know this land and its maps, the relationship to the land is learned, worked and *walked* through Gaelic, its words and phrases, and, through this *languaging* the land rests from technocratic translation.

> For as long is it is supposed that the language, and the traditions encoded therein, can be passed along like a relay baton from generation to generation, it appears to make no difference *where* the people are. (On these grounds, administrations have often seen no principled objection to moving their' indigenous' peoples off the land, or greatly restricting their access, whether in the interests of industrial development or wildlife conservation. It did not occur to them that such displacement might rupture the continuity of tradition or cut the people off from their pasts.) (Ingold, 2000, p. 147)

Translation – the struggle to twist tongues around strange words, the real time grappling for and with words – *is* visceral. When it is not simply a technocratic move it is a languaging response to the world and our relationship with it. It turns our characters inside out and it turns them on to each other and to the land and to other ways of speaking and listening. It is sensuous, erotic, deeply relational, it requires desire to *entertain* other worlds, other ways of being and working, to be united with them, and to feel the powerful textures of their lives.

'To live in the world is also to inhabit it' says Ingold (2000). 'Thus a way of speaking is also a way of living in the land.' And so we move back to where we began with the problematics of culture and the attempt, here, at seeing what translation might look like, or how it might be practised, when it begins from the middle, as Williams (2000) puts it, from the midst of our living in translated worlds. When the genealogies of cultural transmission are prised open and allowed to breathe, when the breeze sweeps away the dust, we might find a broader set of possibilities for conceiving of language and translation than those afforded by our common theorising on language and culture:

> Far from serving as a common currency for the exchange of otherwise private, mental representations, language celebrates an embodied knowledge of the world that is already shared thanks to people's mutual involvement in the task of habitation. It is not, then, language *per se* that ensures the continuity of tradition. Rather it is the tradition of living in the land that ensures the continuity of language. (Ingold, 2000, p. 147)

Translation is implicated in this process of traditioning (Brueggemann, 2003). For Thomas, in *A Sparrow's Flight*, memory and imagination keep alive the knowledge of the names of the hills so that when his people return from their long exile, the names are fresh and fit like a glove. The words lingered in exile, and then came back to explode into life.

Taskscape of the translator: the geopoetics of a speckled-scape

'The relational model, in short, renders difference not as diversity but as positionality. In the relational model "kinship is geography"' (Ingold, 2000, p. 149). And such a relational, positioned view of land, languaging and translation does not make for clean and easily negotiable places. It is not language as tidy, it does not seek to mend the broken middle or translate in such a way as to render it holy, transcendental. It builds in the middle of the world, not from the margins, or from the centre, just from its position, from the inhabited place. The *taskscape* that emerges is speckled, patchy, variegated.

> *Taim ag taisteal trén taisteal trén bhfearann breacis tá dhá ainm ar gach aon bhaile ann. (I am travelling through the speckled land and every town there has two names.)* (Colm Breathnach, 1992)

Under the relational mode translation becomes a source of knowledge and the task of the translator (Benjamin, 1973) is to make sense of the encounters on our path and create what Ingold terms a *taskscape* that grows out of the feelings of relation, the sensory perception of human and non-human phenomena. To dwell or to move along trails, with others, in the taskscape of translation requires what de Certeau (1984) terms 'tactics' – 'a calculated action determined by the absence of a proper locus' as opposed to 'strategies', which he views as Cartesian in attitude; 'an effort to delimit one's own place in a world bewitched by the invisible power of the Other'.

> [...] a tactic boldly juxtaposes diverse elements in order to produce a flash shedding a different light on the language of a place and to strike the hearer. (de Certeau, 1984, pp. 37–38)

This taskscape of translation, this position in the middle of land and life from which languaging begins, placed firmly and squarely in the midst of things yet not requiring or even possessing a locus of power, has been the focus of translation theory from Ireland in particular. Rather than seeing the taskscape of translation as one in which the translator is rendered invisible (Venuti, 1995) Irish theorists of translation view the land as a speckled land, the people, a speckled people (Colm Breathnach, 1992). This idea goes back to much earlier translation antecedents such as the *Leabhar Bhreac* – the Speckled book and the illicit translations by Collum Cille – Columba, which led, indirectly to the founding of the Abbey on Iona and to the spread of Christianity through Scotland and the North of England.

The taskscape, then becomes a *speckled scape*. It is not devoid of the effects and instruments of varieties of power, of history and other agencies. Nor does it use its linguistic and other technologies to strive for uniformity. It is pocked, marked, freckled, and speckled. In times of technocratic translation and what is termed variously, and emotively as both linguistic imperialism (Phillipson, 1992) and linguistic genocide (Skutnabb-Kangas, 2000), it is affords a place for tactical translation actions and for languaging, for a kind of poetic activism of relation. 'Glaramara' says Naomi ... 'Earth' says Marie ... 'Machiare Bhuide' says Yolland ... 'Beinn Vrackie' – say I.

Neither necessarily foreignising nor domesticating, neither 'mouse nor rat', neither constructing nor colonising – though also all of these have their place, but a sensory mode of speckled being, responding and learning to language, inhabiting and building in a world where the locus of power may be elsewhere, but where tactics are suggested by a relationship to the taskscape, to the land and to language. Tactics do not try – indeed cannot aspire to erase or to celebrate the differences, or to build and inhabit something that is other than speckled. They will always be partial, provisional and broken, and even beautiful. When we build in and inhabit the world we do so provisionally – our institutions are imperfect but (Rose, 1992) this does not mean that we do not try. There are clear notes here of Gerald Manley Hopkin's poem *Pied Beauty*: 'Glory be to God for dappled things [...] Landscape plotted and pieced – fold, fallow and plough'.

The taskscape – the hills laid out in front of a friend who is seeing them for the first time – prompts the task, the hard common task of translation as action in the world, and as languaging action. The idea of the taskscape of the translator enables us to see this scape as growing out of feeling and its embodiments, its vitality, its connexity (Cronin, 2002a) and to see the translator as one positioned in the geopoetics of the environment out of which she translates.

> [...] our human cities remain shockingly alive in their plurality of sight and speech. It is Thursday in November and the city of Stockholm is drenched in brightness. Water and bridges and the faded ochres of Venice on wood and stone. There is Swedish on the streets and in the shops. Two of my companions speak Dutch, the third is a Norwegian translator. The variousness of the world seems inexhaustible on a morning like this and Babel a miracle of particulars. Kenneth White speaks of the geopoetic adventure, the discovery of an elsewhere within and without. Here in the blanched sunlight, on the flagstones of a city fading to loveliness, languages and memory mingle in the sustained, enduring wonderwork of human geopoetics. (Cronin, 2000, p. 157)

The task of the translator is the complex task of relating. It is a geopoetic task, as embodying feeling. It has to find ways of working, of languaging not accurately but empathically, poetically, interagentically. It does not need to render one culture in the terms of another or one language in terms of another, it has to work synaesthetically so that a colour may sound and a sound may taste, because 'the ash tree is cold to look at' (Heaney).

Acknowledgements

I wish to acknowledge kind invitations from the University of Cornell, the Open University, the University of Edinburgh and the Coniston Institute, where versions of the paper have been presented. Awol Allo prepared the translation in Amharic, with assistance from Elias Nour, University of Addis Ababa. Katja Frimberger prepared the German translation.

Citations from Friel's *Translations* and from Elphinstone's *A Sparrow's Flight* are cited under fair use and permission has been sought from both the publisher and author respectively.

References

Bassnett, S., & Lefevere, A. (1998). *Constructing cultures: Essays on literary translation.* Clevedon: Multilingual Matters.

Baudelaire, C. (1972). *Les fleurs du mal.* Paris: Editions Gallimard.

Benjamin, W. (1973). *Illuminations.* London: Fontana.

Breathnach, C. (1992). *An fearann breac.* Dublin: Coiscéim.

Brueggemann, W. (2003). *An introduction to the Old Testament: The canon and Christian imagination.* Louisville, KY: Westminster John Knox Press.

Clifford, J. (1997). *Routes: Travel and translation in the late twentieth century.* Cambridge, MA: Harvard University Press.

Cronin, M. (2000). *Across the lines: Travel, language and translation.* Cork: Cork University Press.

Cronin, M. (2002a). 'Thou shalt be one with the birds': Translation, connexity and the New Global Order. *Language and Intercultural Communication, 2*(2), 86–95.

Cronin, M. (2002b). Babel's standing stones: Language, translation and the exosomatic. *Crossings, 2*(1), 1–7.

de Certeau, M. (1984). *The practice of everyday life.* Los Angeles and London: University of California Press.

Deleuze, G., & Guattari, F. (1988). *A thousand plateaux: Capitalism and schizoprenia.* London: Athlone.

Eagleton, T. (2000). *The idea of culture.* Oxford: Blackwell.

Eagleton, T. (2003). *After theory.* London: Penguin.

Elphinstone, M. (1989). *A sparrow's flight: A novel of a future.* Edinburgh: Polygon.

Friel, B. (1981). *Translations.* London: Faber and Faber.

Gormley, A. (2005). An Interview with Anthony Gormley, *Third Way*, March, p. 17.

Hopkins, G.M. (1918). 'Pied Beauty', in *The poems of Gerald Manley Hopkins.* London: Humphrey Milford.

Ingold, T. (1993). The art of translation in a continuous world. In G. Pálsson (Ed.), *Beyond boundaries: Understanding, translation and anthropological discourse* (pp. 210–230). Oxford: Berg.

Ingold, T. (2000). *The perception of the environment: Essays in livelihood, dwelling and skill.* London & New York: Routledge.

Ingold, T. (2011). *Being alive: Essays on movement, knowledge and description.* London: Routledge.

Keesing, R. M. (1994). Radical cultural difference: Anthropology's myth? In M. Pütz (Ed.), *Language contact and language conflict* (pp. 3–24). Amsterdam & Philadelphia: John Benjamins.

Phillipson, R. (1992). *Linguistic imperialism.* Oxford: Blackwell.

Phipps, A., & Gonzalez, M. (2004). *Modern languages: Learning and teaching in an intercultural field.* London: Sage.

Rilke, R.M. (1985). *Die Sonnette an Orpheus.* Frankfurt am Main: Suhrkamp.

Rose, G. (1992). *The broken middle: Out of our ancient society.* Oxford: Blackwell.

Rose, G. (1996). *Mourning becomes the law.* Cambridge: Cambridge University Press.

Skutnabb-Kangas, T. (2000). *Linguistic genocide in education – or worldwide diversity and human rights?* Mahwah, NJ: Lawrence Erlbaum.

Venuti, L. (1995). *The translator's invisibility: A history of translation.* London & New York: Routledge.

Williams, R. (2000). *On Christian theology.* Oxford: Blackwell.

Portuguese 'to go': language representations in tourist guides

Maria João Cordeiro

Instituto Politécnico de Beja, Portugal; CECC - Centro de Estudos de Comunicação e Cultura da Universidade Católica Portuguesa, Lisboa, Portugal

Language difference is an intrinsic aspect of any kind of mobility and especially of tourism, the world's allegedly largest industry which develops around a myriad of multilingual and multicultural places.

However, multilingualism and the intense intermingling of languages characterizing tourist sites are considered a potentially chaos-creating factor by the travel and tourism industry, which has developed around monolingual and linguistically encapsulating paths and settings. Interestingly enough, this development has simultaneously been accompanied by the celebration of polyglossia. The illusion of frictionless linguistic cohesion in a multilingual world is not only constructed by the universal use of English as lingua franca; it is also largely constructed by the transformation of languages into easily and fast acquirable articles to be used by travellers.

A huge ever-increasing language-learning industry flourishes around tourist fluxes: additionally to language sections included in guidebooks there is a profusion of pocket language guides, 'essential guides', 'mini dictionaries', 'phrase books', 'conversation guides' in all possible languages.

The present paper aims at reflecting on the way languages are portrayed in such texts deliberately conceived for people on the move. It focuses, in particular, on Portuguese and the way it is framed in contemporary tourist guides.

As diferenças linguísticas são um aspecto intrínseco de qualquer tipo de mobilidade, especialmente do turismo, alegadamente a maior indústria mundial, que pressupõe uma infinitude de lugares multilingues e multiculturais.

Contudo, o multilinguismo e a intensa mistura de línguas que caracterizam os locais turísticos são considerados pela indústria turística um factor potenciador do caos, motivo pelo qual aquela se tem desenvolvido sobretudo a partir de trajectos e cenários monolingues. Este desenvolvimento tem sido, porém, simultaneamente acompanhado pela celebração do multilinguismo. A ilusão de coesão e fluidez linguísticas num mundo multilingue não é apenas construída através do uso universal do inglês como língua franca, mas também através da transformação de qualquer língua em artigo de aquisição fácil e rápida. A indústria da aprendizagem de línguas estrangeiras floresce à custa dos fluxos turísticos e da sua necessidade de mediação cultural e de preparação linguística: além das secções incluídas em guias turísticos, há uma profusão de mini dicionários e guias de conversação em todas as línguas possíveis.

O presente artigo tem por objectivo reflectir sobre a forma como as línguas são representadas nesse tipo de textos deliberadamente concebidos para viajantes, concentrando-se, em particular, na língua portuguesa e na forma como esta é representada em guias contemporâneos.

Introduction: language and the mobile world

Mobility is a major phenomenon in today's world and it is one of the most highlighted concepts of the academic debate on the contemporary globalized world (Appadurai, 1996; Clifford, 1997; Cresswell, 2009; Urry, 1999). Everything travels today – from living bodies to objects, from images and symbols to ideas, from information and technologies to money – producing what anthropologist Appadurai (1996) has called ethnoscapes, mediascapes, technoscapes, financescapes and ideoscapes.

The movements across languages and cultures inherent to these *scapes* are of utmost importance. They remain, however, absent in Appadurai's discussion and characterization of today's global flows. In fact, the great majority of critical literature on mobility overlooks this crucial dimension of human migrations: the language phenomena, the communication and interaction issues intrinsically involved in the multiple and ever-increasing flows of people on the move around the globe, which create unprecedented opportunities for intercultural encounters and linguistic experiences.

In a recent text on the production of mobilities, sociologist Tim Cresswell (2009) provides a six-themed reflection on the motives, speeds, rhythms, directions, experiences and frictions of mobilities. Cresswell expands on the physicality of mobilities, leaving aside the intangibility of linguistic production inherent to them. A seventh theme on mobilities might be language, linguistic performance, friction and conflict occurring in experiences of displacement and cosmopolitanism, in practices of border-crossing, intercultural contacts and interactions in contemporary social life.

James Clifford's (1997) influential concept of 'travelling cultures' is a major trope of the debate on contemporariness. It questions the conventional idea of 'isomorphism of space, place, and culture' (Gupta & Ferguson, 1992, p. 7) and raises the question that it is no longer possible to conceptualize cultures as space-bounded, united to and inscribed in specific localities, i.e. 'in relation to a fixed, cartographically coordinated space' (Lury, 1997, p. 75). Clifford's reflection reinforces the idea that people do not simply move across an ordered space, entering and getting out of 'places', which supposedly remain untouched in their localized and emblematic distinctiveness. Cultures can be 'tried out' and experienced beyond their assumed 'natural' borders; travellers carry with them their own cultures, their own frames of mind with which they produce meaning and conceptualize the world as they progress on their routes; and in their travels they are also exposed to diversified, sometimes intriguing, puzzling or inspiring soundscapes of wholly different linguistic systems.

Human migration is also therefore to be understood not only as a flow of cultures, but also as a flow of languages. Language differences are an intrinsic consequence of the act of travel, and language plays a crucial role in the way we simply progress geographically and perceive the world and others.

Travellers are not only bodies in transit, performers of ritualized acts, they are language speakers, uttering their native sounds as they move across space, stepping out of their familiar tongues and hesitantly or adventurously articulating foreign words as they consume places and cultures. Images and symbols, information and ideas circulate globally through permanent but apparently invisible translation and communication processes. Globalization has not only led to the hegemony of a lingua franca, but also to a growing awareness of language barriers and cultural diversity. Multilingual and multicultural places proliferate, in the words of travel writer Pico Iyer, in an increasingly 'small and mongrel world', 'where more and more countries are as polyglot and restless as airports' (London, 2011). The intensity and speed at which languages currently travel, co-exist and intermingle might account for a further significant flow that could be termed as *languagescapes*.

The notion of traveling cultures has received increased interest and fructified in the debate around the contemporary world; the notion of mobile languages and the underlying ubiquitous processes of translation in the travel experience clearly lack sufficient debate (Cronin, 2000, p. 102). Given the scale and intensity of current mobilities, but also considering some political discourses on the relevance of multilingualism and some language policies (e.g. Europe and its discourse on European identity grounded on its cultural and multilingual diversity), it is only surprising that similar attention has not been paid to the travelling condition of languages.

The present paper aims at making a contribution to this field of research, by addressing the neglected issue of the role of language(s) in a mobile world, increasingly characterized by multilingual and multicultural encounters. It focuses in particular on language representations disseminated by texts deliberately conceived for linguistic performances in tourism – one of the most celebrated sites of intercultural communication, which requires a closer consideration of the way it actually deals with language and communication.

Multilingualism and the intense intermingling of languages characterizing tourist sites are considered a potentially chaos-creating factor by the travel and tourism industry, which has developed around monolingual and linguistically encapsulating paths and settings. Interestingly enough, this development has simultaneously been accompanied by the celebration of polyglossia. While tourism with its industrial and global mechanisms is highly dependent on a lack of communicative friction and has developed around monolingual paths, it has fed, on the other hand, on cultural and linguistic diversity, by promoting mythical discourses on cultural distinctiveness and more importantly perhaps on smooth intercultural exchanges between so-called 'hosts and guests'.

The paper thus aims to expose the intrinsic linguistic tension lying at the heart of tourist mobilities, which opposes the fleeting and transient character of tourist experiences and encounters to the time-consuming undertaking of language acquisition and intercultural interaction. This tension is significantly downplayed by a text genre which exuberantly grows in the book market for the alleged benefit of people on the move: guidebooks, language guides and phrase books are every traveller's best companion. A huge language-learning industry flourishes around tourists' need for cultural mediation and preparation for different linguistic spaces: additionally to language sections included in guidebooks, there is a profusion of pocket language guides, 'essential guides', 'mini dictionaries', 'phrase books', 'conversation guides' in all possible languages.

The paper finishes by drawing on examples from Portuguese language guides and phrase books, in order to characterize the way they promote the illusion of frictionless mobility – across languages and cultures – and to ultimately unpack the paradox between the process of language commodification in tourism and its alleged goal of promoting intercultural communication and understanding.

Tourist encounters, languages, guidebooks and phrase books

The tourist encounter with locals is probably one of the most imagined and mythified moments of travel experiences. Many tourists travel to get to know and be in contact with other peoples and cultures. The myth of tourism as a major site of intercultural communication is grounded on the idea that travelling promotes understanding and close exchanges between tourists and hosts. In fact, the success of travel is very often identified with the possibility of engaging with local populations and, to a large extent, of becoming oneself, albeit temporarily, 'the other'.

Many of the strategies for this cultural immersion involve practices and performances for not being or appearing to be a tourist, such as hiding the camera and/or the guidebook, taking the public bus, going to 'typical' restaurants, avoiding organized tours and the hallmarks of tourism, seeking off-the-beaten-track paths. The ability to speak the local language is probably the ultimate strategy to fit in to the local landscape. To speak a local language is somehow to play at being a local, to escape temporarily from one's own too familiar world and thus forge a whole new identity. Not to speak the local language or to have a poor command of the foreign language potentially implies a wide spectrum of interactional dramas and linguistic struggles, often accompanied by a discomforting feeling of helplessness. Most tourist encounters emerge from attempts to deal with everyday needs and concerns, such as ordering food, getting on the right metro line or finding the way back to the hotel. Surviving in an unfamiliar environment and making one's way through various linguistic negotiations lie at the heart of every tourist's anxieties. 'Culture shock', as Pearce (2005, p. 130) notes, entails an expanded range of complexities that goes beyond the mere spatial disorientation or physical difficulties resulting, for example, from time changes or different food; an important component of the phenomenon resides in potentially stressful 'communication challenges'. Travelling to another country and moving across cultures represent almost always destabilizing experiences of vulnerability and crisis, which, in the worst possible cases, can turn tourists/ travellers into 'a mute presence in a world of foreign [disorienting and threatening] signs', producing the 'relational tragedy of autism', for they can never really come out of the enclosure they find themselves in without being able to engage with others (Cronin, 2000, p. 35).

The tourism industry has dealt with the intrinsic babelic nature of travelling in two apparently antagonistic main ways: on the one hand, it has stimulated the growth of risk-reducing infrastructures for travellers, what Cronin (2000) calls 'the monoglossic bubble of international tourism', in which the universal use of English as lingua franca, as Cronin (2000) notes, has created the illusion of a frictionless monoglossia and linguistic homogeneity. These bubbles include so-called 'enclavic spaces', e.g. airports, train stations, hotels and resorts, museums and heritage sites, theme parks and guided tours within or between attractions (Edensor, 2000). These spaces are self-contained and carefully regulated and managed, allowing for very little or no contact at all between tourists and local populations or residents. Tourists perform according to previously set rules and directions, hardly ever stepping into the chaotic and uncontrolled environments of local life (Edensor, 2000).

On the other hand, though, the development of the monoglossic paths of international tourism and its consequent linguistic encapsulation of tourists have also stimulated a huge language-learning industry, providing tourists with a diversified range of linguistic tools allegedly created to facilitate and promote the interaction with hosts, i.e., linguistic tools that, in fact, instigate tourists to break through the bubble and effectively take a plunge into the chaos of local life.

A large language-learning industry exuberantly grows for the alleged benefit of tourist–host relationships. A quick survey of some of the titles and series offered by the most well-known publishing houses specialized in phrase books and language guides provides an elucidating idea of how foreign-language learning is promoted as an easy, fast and effortless undertaking. Dorling Kindersley, for example, proposes a wide range of 15-minute eyewitness travel language guides. By practising 'just 4 times a week for 3 months', with 'no writing or homework', a 'revolutionary new system that makes learning quick, easy and fun' allows you to learn to speak and understand the foreign language with confidence (whether it is Italian, Spanish, Japanese or Chinese; whether 'starting from scratch or just in need of a refresher').[1] Berlitz publishing employs a similar seductive rhetoric to convey smooth, quick and comfortable linguistic and cultural acquisition. Phrase books are praised as 'lightweight, portable packs', providing the traveller 'with the key phrases to get the most out of [the] trip' – everyday phrases that every traveler needs'; the range 'Berlitz for your trip' aims at 'effortlessly' teaching 'all the essential phrases', 'in a no-stress, all audio, completely portable format, ideal for learning on-the-go'.[2]

Phrase books promote the fiction of fast language learning and instantaneous communicative success, fully enacting Zygmunt Bauman's (2000) well-known metaphor of 'liquidity', used to characterize the contemporary speeded-up world. The possibility of moving faster both physically and virtually between places today seems to have found correspondence in language learning through the celebrated apparent possibility of moving quickly, effortlessly and pleasurably across languages and cultures.

Cultural immersion 'into the other' is another recurrent promise of error-free linguistic achievements: getting a phrase book is apparently half way to 'fail-safe small talk', to speaking 'with aplomb', 'like a local' or 'chatting faux-pas free'.[3] In these phrase books, the encounter with the impenetrable sounds of actually spoken languages is framed by a fiction of easy and comfortable linguistic performance, which ignores the complex and messy dimension of orality and the painful bodily sensations involved in utterance efforts, speech production and pronunciation (Phipps, 2007). As Phipps (2007, p. 95) further sustains, pronunciation is 'the first stage in detaching from one language and understanding another' and corresponds to a 'bodily phenomenon', an attempt at living fully, "humanely' in the tourist world'.

Downplaying potential pronunciation problems lies, in fact, at the core of the foreign-language-learning world fictionalized by phrase books. Correct pronunciation seems to be the key to local talk, as illustrated by the following examples from Lonely Planet phrase books:

> Creaky high tones and aspirated consonants have never been so easy! Nor has requesting your favourite song at a karaoke bar, chatting to a monk, or bargaining with your cabbie. With our easy-to-use phrase book to guide you'll be talking up a storm with the locals in no time.[4]

> Learning the Fijian language means you can get away from the tourist areas and out into the real Fiji – where a little bit of local talk goes a long way.[5]

The national language of Malaysia is a surprisingly easy language to wrap your tongue around. Words are largely pronounced phonetically – so dive in and leave that language barrier in the dust.[6]

Portuguese 'to go'

The present section aims at looking closer into such 'languages to go' (an expression borrowed from a language-learning series called Living Language, published by Random House[7]). It focuses on a limited sample of the language sections of Portugal guidebooks and also on Portuguese phrase books, targeted at speakers of French, German, Spanish and English. Sample selection considered not only texts by major and renowned publishing houses with a widespread reputation in travel guides (such as Lonely Planet and Baedeker), but also their current availability and likelihood to be acquired and actually used by tourists visiting Portugal. The analysis could not obviously aim at being exhaustive or at providing definite conclusions for the whole language-learning or guidebook industry. It sought to argue that it is possible to find evidence for the fact that, irrespective of the linguistically different audiences they try to reach, guidebook language sections and phrase books typically share mechanisms of language portrayal, resorting to common categories, fixed formulas and sets of requests and answers, that ultimately envision language learning as an automatic and effortless process aimed at apparently just catering for tourists' linguistic needs.

The text analysis first focused on the way the Portuguese language is generally perceived, looking for keywords and common semantic areas used to characterize and describe it. Secondly, the analysis moved on to identify categories around which language portrayal is organized and to reveal how 'guests' and 'hosts' relations are linguistically framed, imagined and depicted.

Language perception: Portuguese as a mysterious, difficult and formal language

Guidebooks and phrase books tend to start by presenting a brief characterization of the local language, establishing relationships with and analogies to other languages; unsurprisingly, the analysed texts share the same well-established ideas – or perhaps what we might call, evoking Laurie Bauer's and Peter Trudgill's book (1998), the same 'myths'.

They underline the written similarities with Spanish, as well as the differences and difficulties in spoken Portuguese. In some guidebooks and phrase books, we find the idea that oral Portuguese is a mysterious and difficult language with a complex sound system, which includes sibilants, nasal sounds, diphthongs, and swallowed word endings. A difference between European and Brazilian Portuguese is also generally established:

> High-school Spanish may help with signs and menus, but will not unlock the mysteries of spoken Portuguese. The Portuguese in Portugal is much more closed and guttural-sounding, and is also spoken much faster than in Brazil. (*Berlitz Pocket Guide Portugal*, 2010, p. 169)

Guidebooks and phrase books for German and English speakers emphasize e.g. the fact that oral Portuguese hardly resembles a Romance language, stating that it recalls a Slavic tongue or even Russian:

> Although similar to Spanish in its written form, Portuguese sounds very different. In fact, it is not easy to recognize spoken Portuguese as a Romance language, and many people have compared its sound to Russian. (Poelzl, 2009, p. 207)

Another aspect pointed out by guidebooks and phrase books is the language's outstanding formality. They provide interesting considerations about the Portuguese forms of greetings and address. The phrase book for Spanish-speaking people, for instance, underlines the fact that:

> The Portuguese are exquisitely well-educated and courteous and they expect to be treated in that same way. They respect the forms of address and formulas of courtesy and they do it with notable smoothness and delicacy. (*Portugués para viajar*, 2010, p. 6, my translation)

Overall, the perception of the Portuguese language seems to oscillate between exoticism and familiarity, trying to provide a seductive balance between challenging (but minor) difficulties and tranquilizing similarities.

Linguistic reassurance – preventing muteness

Guidebooks and phrase books generally care for the linguistic reassurance of their readers, referring to the skills of the Portuguese in foreign-language speaking, especially in the language of their readership. Language learners and would-be tourists are reassured that they will not be speechless in Portugal and will be able to understand and above all to be understood.

The Lonely Planet Portugal guidebook maintains that 'nearly all Turismo staff in Portugal speak some English' and that 'some in the service industry, like waiters and baristas, may insist on showing their English skills, despite your attempts to stick to Portuguese' (Landon & St. Louis, 2007, p. 481).

Similarly, the Baedeker Portugal guidebook (*Portugal. Baedeker Allianz Reiseführer*, 2006, p. 149) stresses the absence of any communication problems in hotels and major restaurants, and the French guidebook declares that speaking Portuguese is not indispensable to 'get by' in Lisbon: 'Rassurez-vous, la connaissance du portugais n'est cependant pas indispensable pour vous débrouiller à Lisbonne' (Montagnon, 2008, p. 198).

Portuguese soundscapes are apparently a major concern for speakers of other languages and a source of potential anxiety. So, even if the pronunciation difficulties are overtly declared, they are also immediately downplayed and counterbalanced by familiar traits:

> The main challenge of Portuguese pronunciation for English speakers are the characteristic nasal sounds. Most other phonemes are similar to those in English. (Poelzl, 2009, p. 208)

The meaningfulness of learning the local language

After reassuring their readers that speaking Portuguese is not indispensable to get by in Portugal, guidebooks and phrase books move on to encouraging the learning of the local language, relating it and the subsequent possibility of conversing with local populations to a rewarding experience. Some elucidating examples:

Anyone can speak another language! It's all about confidence. (...) Even if you learn the very basics (...), your travel experience will be the better for it. You have nothing to lose and everything to gain when the locals hear you making an effort. (*Lonely Planet Portuguese Phrase Book,* 2006, p. 4)

Open this book and take the plunge – Portuguese is the key to an adventure of your own. (*Lonely Planet Portuguese Phrase Book,* 2006, back cover)

Living in a foreign country and having little or no contact with the locals is a missed opportunity. (...) By getting to know the locals, you will gain a better understanding of the Portuguese people and their culture, which will immensely enrich your time in Portugal. (Poelzl, 2009, p. 117)

Similarly, the French tourist guide sustains that 'obviously all your efforts to speak the language will always be appreciated' (Montagnon, 2008, p. 198, my translation). The German Marco Polo language guide, significantly entitled 'Never again speechless!', announces on its opening page, much in line with the myth of tourism as a site of intercultural communication, that 'words connect, words unveil new worlds, words simply let you live more' (*Portugiesisch – Nie mehr sprachlos,* 2009, my translation).

A Lilliputian language version

Language guides present astonishingly compact and apparently easy-to-acquire versions of the languages they promote: this is clearly conveyed by the Lilliputian dimensions of most language guides, conceived to be discretely consulted and rapidly hidden into one's pocket.

However linguistically different their target public might be, phrase books and language sections of guidebooks are very similarly organized: language is as if chopped in distinct blocks, 'manageable chunks' (Jack & Phipps, 2005, p. 86), sorted out by categories. Table 1 lists the main categories of information gathered in the analyzed guidebooks and phrase books.

Each one of the different categories corresponds mainly to 'transactional' contexts, in which tourists are likely to find themselves: service encounters, in which tourists primarily seek to satisfy their human needs, to solve their problems, to

Table 1.   Main categories of information gathered from scrutinized guidebooks and phrase books.

Categories	Contents
'Essentials' or 'basics'	pronunciation, the alphabet, numbers, amounts, times and dates; basic grammar issues; everyday expressions;
Socializing	greetings, small talk, meetings, romance/pick-up lines, expressing opinions, understanding problems, 'local talk'
Transports	getting around, asking for directions
Food	eating out, menu guides, food glossaries, ordering a meal
Services and shopping	at the bank, post office, hairdresser
Accommodation	at the hotel, making reservations
Safe travel	health, at the doctor
Leisure	sports, outdoor activities

provide for their well-being, and to minimize any risk of identity loss through language loss. The main point is, as the Spanish phrase book states, that tourists make themselves understood. These texts contain listings of such phrases as: 'Is it safe to swim here?' (*Eyewitness Travel Guides Portuguese Phrase Book,* 2003, p. 82); 'I have lost a filling' (*Eyewitness Travel Guides Portuguese Phrase Book,* 2003, p. 101); 'Podría indicarme un buen restaurante?' [Could you recommend a good restaurant?] (*Portugués para viajar,* 2010, p. 44); 'Can I kiss you?' (*Lonely Planet Portuguese Phrase Book*, 2006, p. 127); 'Könnten Sie bitte ein Foto von uns machen?' [Could you take a picture of us?] (*PONS Sprachführer Portugiesisch – Alles für die Reise,* 2010, p. 141). These examples only highlight the attempt to master the appropriate language needed to attenuate tourist anxieties. They aim at being veritable linguistic 'survival kits'.

Language is reduced to lists of 'keywords', structures and phrases. The interactional dimensions of true conversation and exchange – its unpredictability and spontaneity are, of course, totally absent. Dialogues are artificially construed upon a previously established set of expected questions (centred around the traveller's needs), often followed by locals' ideal (unreal?) responses. One innovative but innocuous attempt to bring the local into the dialogue refers to the inclusion of sections pointing to the 'Things you'll hear' (*DK Eyewitness guide*) or 'Listen for . . .' (*Lonely Planet phrase book*). For the most part, however, as Thurlow and Jaworski declare, the 'local person remains (. . .) 'unspoken' and unknown' (Thurlow & Jaworski, 2010, p. 217).

It could, in fact, be said that this 'Portuguese to go' – as any other language for tourist purposes – has been, in fact, subject to what might be called tourism's 'miniaturising technique' (González, 2007), a phenomenon typically depicted by tourist art and souvenirs. Places' souvenirization corresponds to a process of coping with the world's complexity, reducing it to a few identifiable symbols. Susan Stewart (1993) has referred to how the reduction in physical dimensions corresponds to an increase in significance, the encapsulation of life, the eternalization of an environment 'by closing it off from the possibility of lived experience' (Stewart, 1993, p. 144).

A similar process seems to occur in these phrasebooks and guidebooks, which produce 'toy versions' of languages, encapsulating and eternalizing them in fixed, artificial interactions, from which all unpredictability characterizing human communication is removed. As Thurlow (cited in Thurlow & Jaworski, 2010, p. 213) notes about guidebook glossaries, for example, they 'promote the literal and denotative, the formulaic and reductive, at the expense of the subtle, the complex, the messy, the 'lived'', by disembedding them from any 'cultural context of any plausible, extended tourist-host relationship' (Thurlow & Jaworski, 2010, p. 216); they are intended for the tourist to 'get by', hardly leading to truly 'language autonomy'.

Phrase books especially designed for travellers with their selections within the contexts of mobility are a kind of miniaturized representations of languages, from which 'all human labour and suffering' involved in translation, learning and oral speech in lived context 'magically disappear' (González, 2007). Phrase books have the same materiality as souvenirs, conjugating both a material and abstract nature: usually as miniature books themselves (handy pocket-sized booklets), they function as a 'talisman to the body' (Stewart, 1997, p. 41), whose very possession evokes the dreamworld of the symbolic consumption of the other: the taming of the foreign language.

Conclusion

The illusion of linguistic frictionless cohesion in a multilingual world is not only constructed by the universal use of English, it is also largely conveyed by the commodification of languages, by the transformation of languages, including less widely spoken tongues, into easily and fast acquirable articles to be used on the move and in supposedly genuine intercultural interactions.

Tourism has not only transformed cultures, countries, regions and cities into the accessible articles of mobility, in a world, using the appropriate metaphor of historian Schivelbusch (2000), which has become a 'large department store of landscapes and cities'. Tourism has also led to the celebration of polyglossia by providing an overwhelming wide range of textual genres allegedly aimed at preventing and minimizing culture shocks.

Despite the monoglossic bubbles of international tourism, in which everything is always translated into English and the contact between tourists and locals is sometimes reduced to sporadic, fleeting and 'transactional' relations between clients and service providers, between a leisured and a working population, language diversity is overtly promoted and celebrated through an inspiring proliferation of linguistic tools that encourage the learning of local languages, turning them into a crucial aspect of a rewarding and successful travel experience.

A brief analysis of currently available Portugal guidebooks and Portuguese phrase books has attempted to provide evidence on the way language differences and cultural barriers are largely contaminated by the prevailing cultural discourse on the contemporary world of frictionless flows. Language representations are grounded in the seductive fiction of easy and fast foreign-language learning as the key to successful cultural appropriation. As one of the phrase books declares: 'Local knowledge, new relationships and a sense of satisfaction are on the tip of your tongue' (*Lonely Planet Portuguese Phrase Book*, 2006, p. 10).

Phrase books and guidebooks addressing different audiences do not differ significantly from each other, 'chopping' and dividing the Portuguese language into manageable pieces – commodified for the use of would-be tourists; it is neither Portugal nor its culture that are represented through the commodification of its language. Language sections of guidebooks and phrase books for tourist purposes revolve around communicative contexts which are most likely to arise between service providers (hosts) and service seekers (guests); language commodification is about satisfying tourists' needs, about providing them with linguistic guidance and reassurance and above all about conveying the idea that learning the language of a destination is equivalent to a meaningful cultural immersion: through speaking a foreign language – even in its formulaic and reduced version – the tourist engages in the illusion of fitting in the landscape and trying out a different identity.

Language representations in tourist guides correspond to a fictionalization process, which is central to tourism's representational dynamics in general. Tourism revolves around cultural appropriation through symbolic consumption; otherness is depicted and enacted according to prevailing myths and utopias. As some studies on tourist texts have shown (Cordeiro, 2010; Fendl & Löffler, 1992; Gorsemann, 1995), cultural representations of destinations are projections of individual or collective fantasies, hardly corresponding to innocent depictions 'or mere reflections of reality – they are drawn from a stock of cultural knowledge which is itself highly ideological and selective' (Morgan & Pritchard, 1998, p. 241).

Similarly, language representations in tourism apparently do not escape this highly ideological and selective discourse – just like destinations, regions and cities, languages are packaged as simplified versions, compact, fast and easily acquirable articles, to glitter in the global, mediated arena of tourist flows.

Notes

1. http://www.dorlingkindersley-uk.co.uk/nf/Search/AdvSearchProc/1,,S195,00.html (retrieved January 20, 2011).
2. http://www.berlitzbooks.com/berlitz/phrase_books.asp?TAG=&CID (retrieved January 20, 2011).
3. http://shop.lonelyplanet.com/france/french-phrasebook-3 (retrieved January 20, 2011).
4. http://shop.lonelyplanet.com/myanmar-burma/burmese-phrasebook-4 (retrieved January 20, 2011).
5. http://shop.lonelyplanet.com/fiji/fijian-phrasebook-2 (retrieved January 20, 2011).
6. http://shop.lonelyplanet.com/malaysia/malay-phrasebook-3 (retrieved January 20, 2011).
7. http://www.randomhouse.com/livinglanguage/Audio-Scripts/Complete_Courses/ (retrieved January 20, 2011).

References

Appadurai, A. (1996). *Modernity at large: Cultural dimensions of globalization*. Minneapolis: University of Minnesota Press.

Bauer, L., & Trudgill, P. (Eds.). (1998). *Language myths*. London: Penguin Books.

Bauman, Z. (2000). *Liquid modernity*. Cambridge: Polity Press.

Berlitz Pocket Guide Portugal (2010). London: Berlitz Publishing/Apa.

Clifford, J. (1997). *Routes, travel and translation in the late twentieth century*. Cambridge, MA/ London: Harvard University Press.

Cordeiro, M.J. (2010). *Olhares Alemães: Portugal na Literatura Turística. Guias de viagem e artigos de imprensa (1980–2006) [German Gazes: Portugal in tourist literature. Guidebooks and press travel articles]*. Lisbon: Faculdade de Ciências Sociais e Humanas da Universidade Nova de Lisboa/Edições Colibri.

Cresswell, T. (2009). Seis temas na produção das mobilidades [Six themes in the production of mobilities]. In R. do Carmo & J.A. Simões (Eds.), *A produção das mobilidades: redes, espacialidades e trajectos* [The production of mobilities: networks, spacialities and paths] (pp. 25–40). Lisboa: ICS.

Cronin, M. (2000). *Across the lines – travel, language, translation*. Cork: Cork University Press.

Edensor, T. (2000). Staging tourism – tourists as performers. *Annals of Tourism Research, 27*(2), 322–344.

Eyewitness Travel Guides Portuguese Phrase Book (2003). London: Dorling Kindersley.

Fendl, E., & Löffler, K. (1992). Utopiazza – Städtische Erlebnisräume in Reiseführern [Utopiazza – urban spaces in guidebooks]. *Zeitschrift für Volkskunde, 88*, 30–48.

González, F.E. (2007, August 18). Souvenirs y turistas [Souvenirs and tourists]. *El País*.

Gorsemann, S. (1995). *Bildungsgut und touristische Gebrauchsanweisung – Produktion, Aufbau und Funktion von Reiseführern* [Cultural and instructive – the production, structure and function of guidebooks]. Münster/New York: Waxmann.

Gupta, A., & Ferguson, J. (1992). Beyond 'culture': Space, identity, and the politics of difference. *Cultural Anthropology, 7*(1), 6–23.

Jack, G., & Phipps, A. (2005). *Tourism and intercultural exchange – why tourism matters.* Clevedon/Buffalo/Toronto: Channel View Publications.

Landon, R., & St. Louis, R. (2007). *Portugal* (6th ed). London: Lonely Planet.

London, S. (2011). Postmodern tourism: A conversation with Pico Iyer. Retrieved January 25, 2011 from http://www.scottlondon.com/interviews/iyer.html

Lonely Planet Portuguese Phrase Book (2006). Victoria: Lonely Planet.

Lury, C. (1997). The objects of travel. In C. Rojek & J. Urry (Eds.), *Touring cultures – transformations of travel and theory* (pp. 75–95). London/New York: Routledge.

Montagnon, D. (2008). *Lisbonne – guide Évasion.* Paris: Hachette.

Morgan, N., & Pritchard, A. (1998). *Tourism promotion and power: Creating images, creating identities.* Chichester, UK: John Wiley.

Pearce, P.L. (2005). *Tourist behaviour – themes and conceptual schemes.* Clevendon/Buffalo/Toronto: Channel View Publications.

Phipps, A. (2007). *Learning the arts of linguistic survival – languaging, tourism, life.* Clevedon/Buffalo/Toronto: Channel View Publications.

Poelzl, V. (2009). *Culture shock! A survival guide to customs and etiquette: Portugal.* Tarrytown: Marshall Cavendish Editions.

PONS Sprachführer Portugiesisch – Alles für die Reise (2010). Stuttgart: Pons.

Portugal. Baedeker Allianz Reiseführer (2006). Ostfildern: Baedeker.

Portugiesisch – Nie mehr sprachlos! (2009). Ostfildern: Mairdumont.

Portugués para viajar (2010). Madrid: Anaya.

Schivelbusch, W. (2000). *Geschichte der Eisenbahnreise: Zur Industrialisierung von Raum und Zeit im 19. Jahrhundert* [The Railway Journey: the industrialization and perception of space in the 19th century]. Frankfurt am Main: Fischer [Original work published 1977].

Stewart, S. (1993). *On longing – narratives of the miniature, the gigantic, the souvenir, the collection.* Durham and London: Duke University Press.

Thurlow, C., & Jaworski, A. (2010). *Tourism discourse – language and global mobility.* New York: Palgrave Macmillan.

Urry, J. (1999). 'Mobile cultures', published by the Department of Sociology, Lancaster University, Lancaster LA1 4YN, UK. Retrieved January 25, 2011, from http://www.comp.lancs.ac.uk/sociology/papers/Urry-Mobile-Cultures.pdf

'Please don't climb trees and pick flowers for the sake of life' – making sense of bilingual tourism signs in China

Oliver Radtke and Xin Yuan

Cluster of Excellence: Asia and Europe in Global Context, Heidelberg University, Heidelberg, Germany

This paper deals with Chinglish as Chinese-English translations found on public bilingual signage in the People's Republic of China. After a short review of the existing literature, this study attempts to establish a typology of Chinglish with corpus-based research. Additionally, the corpus serves for geographical and statistical analysis. This study finds that the majority of errors are over-literal translations with grammatical mistakes. Only a few signs feature irrelevant wording, Pinyin or typos. Very few signs feature Gibberish with completely unintelligible word fragments or a random set of characters. The problem does not lie with the sign producer, since most of the time the words appear to be correctly copied and stenciled onto a sign surface, the problem lies with the translator. The number of Propaganda Chinglish signs is very low, given the commercial nature of more than 90% of the corpus. Noticeably, more than 80% of the signs carrying non-commercial information or guidance or warnings do not feature the institution, official bureaus or authorities that issued the signs. Tourism is a major contributor of the corpus with about one fourth of the total number of signs. Further research is needed to elaborate on the decorative use of English in the commercial realm, where the existence of non-Chinese lettering is used to establish an appearance of cosmopolitanism or the status of an international brand. The anonymous nature of the communication between the issuing institution and the general public is another striking feature of the present research results.

本文研究中国大陆中英双语标志上的"中式英语"。在评述前人研究的基础上，本文致力于对中式英语图片库的考察以及其类型学和地理分布的考量，以阐述中式英语标志存在的社会原因，从而进一步探究当下中国正在经历的"英语热"的社会意义，以及中国各单位部门通过带有中式英语的双语标识向国际社会展示的中国形象。本研究发现双语标识上的中式英语出现频率最高的特点是带有语法错误的逐字翻译，只有少数的标识上出现无关词汇，拼音和拼写错误，其次，极少数的标识上出现不完整单词和字母等乱码。所以可以推断在标识制作过程中，翻译环节出现问题的可能性最大。另外，政治宣传方面的双语标识非常少，而商用标识占中式英语图片库内容的 90%以上。值得注意的是，其中 80%的带有非商业内容的指导性或者警告性标识没有任何单位署名。由此本文建议在对双语标识的后续研究中，应当着重考量针对以标识上非中文文字的装饰性来树立全球化和国际化形象的现象，以及大多数标识与其受众之间的匿名交流现象。

Introduction

Most China travellers have spotted them, sometimes even while still being at the airport: signs that feature statements such as 'No entry in peacetime' (i.e. No exit except in an emergency), 'Little grass has life – Please watch your step' (i.e. Please do not walk on the grass) in public parks or 'Protect circumstance begins with me' (i.e. Protecting the environment begins here) on a dustbin for recyclable waste. More inscrutable signs include at a lakeside in Suzhou where you are reminded of 'No swimming, fishing or whiffing in the pond', and a public sign titled 'the sweet hint' in Shenyang educates you that 'Grass blue under the foot is forgiving' and urges you: 'Please don't climb trees and pick flowers for the sake of life'. There are also notices that may seem overly explicit to the Anglophone traveller such as the 'Diarrhea clinic' and 'Senyo Anus and Intestine Hospital' in Shanghai, and the massage parlor in Guilin which lures you in with the words 'In here, enjoys under foot. Goes out here, is happy you'.

What is Chinglish anyway, you might ask? The Oxford English Online Dictionary (dictionary.oed.com, 2010) defines Chinglish as

> colloq. (freq. depreciative), a mixture of Chinese and English; esp. a variety of English used by speakers (*sic*) of Chinese or in a bilingual Chinese and English context, typically incorporating some Chinese vocabulary or constructions, or English terms specific to a Chinese context . . ..

In this paper, though, Chinglish is defined, not as a deficient oral usage of English in the process of learning the language, but as an interchangeably creative or plain wrong occurrence on bilingual[1] Chinese-English public signage in the People's Republic of China. Public signage is treated very broadly and includes all kinds of bilingual text that is publicly available,[2] which could appear from commodity packaging to T-Shirts.[3] This paper deals with Chinglish as Chinese-English translations found on public bilingual signage in the People's Republic of China. It begins with a review of the existing literature, which problematizes the partiality of focus of the previous studies and present why this study is necessary. The aim of this study is to establish a typology of Chinglish data with corpus-based research and explains in detail the codification and the meanings of the Chinglish data as well as their roles in Chinese society. Additionally, the corpus also serves for geographical and statistical analysis as another perspective of the sociality of the Chinglish phenomena.

Review of the literature

Scholarly research outside of China on Chinglish is scarce. Previous studies fall into the categories of error analysis, standardization and language history. Zhang (2003) is the only PhD from a non-Chinese university dealing with Chinglish beyond simple quotation of Chinglish examples for humorous effect. She contextualizes Chinglish in a historical review of Chinese Englishes from early Pidgin English to the most recent code-mixing by analyzing a number of representative texts from newspapers, textbooks, and creative writings from Chinese contemporary authors who publish in English.

Pinkham (1998, p. 1) identifies Chinglish on two levels: word choice and sentence structure. The cited materials are mainly from the political genre, such as official documents, or draft versions of newspaper articles that later appeared in *China Daily* and English-language magazines. For Pinkham, who worked as a copy editor in China, 'Chinglish, of course, is that misshapen, hybrid language that is neither English nor Chinese but that might be described as "English with Chinese characteristics."' Pinkham states that 'almost every English text that has been produced by a native speaker of Chinese contains unnecessary words', which she classifies into five categories: (1) unnecessary nouns and verbs; (2) unnecessary modifiers; (3) redundant twins; (4) saying the same thing twice; (5) repeated references to the same thing. Pinkham's study is a useful starting point for this paper, although it did not codify what are the 'Chinese characteristics' in Chinglish; in addition, it is restricted to the realm of newspaper editing and falls short of linking content analysis with statistical and geographical analysis. Furthermore, sign translation is a different endeavor than transferring the meaning of a newspaper article from one language to another. This paper will shed some light on the specific difficulties involved in translating signs.

In the Chinese academic context, research on Chinglish is not abundant either. Lü (Lü & Dan, 2002; Lü & Wang, 2007) is the only researcher who has published monographs on English-Chinese bilingual signs. His focus is on compiling standardized sign lists and dictionaries that serve as a reference compendium. Sociologically or sociolinguistically motivated research is not visible in his studies.

Until December 2010, the Chinese academic papers database Wanfang shuju 万方数据 accessible through the *China Academic Journals* database hosted at Staatsbibliothek Berlin, listed 64 MA and 1 PhD theses dealing with '*Zhongshi yingyu* 中式英语' (Chinglish). Forty-three percent of these theses do *not* come from the current top 100 universities (CUAA, 2010) and the remaining 57% mostly originate in low- or middle-ranked universities in the top 100. Since research on public signage is not necessarily done under the keyword 'Chinglish', another search was done with the term '*gongshiyu* 公示语' (public sign language) and similar results were found: 36% come from universities outside the top 100 with the majority of the remaining 64% originating from low- or middle-ranked universities in the top 100. It would be an exaggeration to conclude that the research quality on Chinglish is low because it is not dealt with at the current top-ranked universities; however, considering that the top 100 universities in China hold an absolute majority of the researchers, research funding, as well as research centers (more than 50% of annual research funding and state key laboratories is centered on the top 34 universities, according to the 2009 press conference report of the Vice Minister of Education), it requires further research to substantially draw conclusions on why Chinglish research does not meet the interests of China's elite universities.

The position of the above-mentioned theses on Chinglish can be summarized as follows: firstly, Chinglish is regarded solely as a problem; it is hindering effective communication with foreign visitors. The English translation on the signs is to be read by foreigners and overseas Chinese who cannot speak Chinese. As stated in the majority of the MA theses referenced above, the authors wish to assist China's rapid economic development and help promote China's international image; and to this end they are searching for effective methods for regulating Chinglish into Standard English. Secondly, most aforementioned previous studies follow a global tendency of advocating bilingual signs as a means of communication and a sign of social sophistication, which strongly suggest that China should follow suit. That is why most of the previous reviewed studies focus on regulation and correction of the

English in signs. Thirdly, most thesis writers are more interested in the response of the foreign receiver; little regard is given to Chinglish as a phenomenon with sociological or sociolinguistic relevance.

Furthermore, when we take a look at the time span in which the *gongshiyu* 公示语 studies were produced, it is reasonable to speculate about a possible influence of the Chinese government on the growing interest in academic research into this topic. There is a steep increase in MA theses produced between 2006 (4) and 2007 (17) with 21 in total, produced in 2008. Thereafter, there is a visible decrease to 13 theses in the following year.[4] It is worth deliberating on a possible connection between the growing number of pragmatic correction-oriented theses and an event that China was highly motivated to present in a flawless fashion: the 29th Olympic Games in Beijing. This hypothesis is indicated by the drastic change in numbers after 2008, when the public interest (and the interest of the Western media) shifted away from bilingual signage to other pressing topics in China.

What conclusions can be drawn from this set of data? Research on Chinglish is certainly not as faulty as a huge number of public bilingual signs, but it also does not rank very high on the nationwide academic agenda either, which is reflected by the lack of interest in this topic amongst the top 100 universities. It might be speculated, as Radtke (2010) puts it, that research was pushed when it was necessary to deliver pragmatic, correction-oriented statements from academia on how to improve the nation's public bilingual signage standard, and was off-stage again when the Olympics and Paralympics were over. For many local and central governmental offices, presenting the country in a flawless bilingual manner has become an industry of its own. In May 2005 the *China Daily* website, as reported by the China Education and Research Network, held a press conference to announce a campaign on 'Use Accurate English to Welcome the Olympics – Public Bilingual Sign Standardization Drive' at Beijing's University of International Business and Economics (Anonymous, 2005). The *Beijing Speaks Foreign Languages Committee*, run by Beijing Municipality, issued month-long correction campaigns to eradicate Chinglish. Similar acts were carried out before the Shanghai EXPO. A campaign to replace Chinglish (or 'shocking English, *leiren yingyu* 雷人英语' as the site called it, using a popular youth term) from street signs has been online since April 2010 with prizes such as free online English courses. The latest campaign was held in Guangzhou in November last year in preparation for the 2010 Asian Games.

The complete list of the above-mentioned small selection of official campaigns and activities is long; changes are clearly visible in China's metropolitan cities but, as the growing number of picture contributions to Facebook's photo group 'Chinglish – save China's disappearing culture' or Flickr's photo pools shows, Chinglish is far from becoming extinct, thus questioning the effectiveness of the above listed governmental acts.

About this study

If it is not about a pragmatic focus on translation theory and correction, how should Chinglish be approached? As Radtke (2010) states, the focus on pragmatic translation correction and patriotic contribution to the motherland's progress is not matched by an equal interest in the exploration of the multi-layered meaning that is behind Chinglish, whose very existence is a statement about contemporary China concerning her current and historic relationship with the West. The daily Chinglish production is a meaningful set of data from a sociolinguistic point of view. The analysis of Chinglish as an application of the Bourdieusian sense of 'capital' is a helpful auxiliary discourse for a partial analysis of contemporary Chinese society. And finally, the production and the official battle against Chinglish is a rich source for analyzing governmental administrative processes.

Research on Chinglish needs to be considered within the context of an existing English fever (*yingyu re* 英语热) in China, which has been growing out of China's Reform and Opening-up Policy in 1978 and into a highly profitable industry of English language teaching and training.[5] The Reform and Opening-up Policy in 1978 featured the abolition of people's communes, the remittance of family-oriented agriculture, and the limited introduction of prices and markets, in order to stimulate production via natural market regulation for the establishment of a socialist market economy with Chinese features. The results of reform and opening-up policies not only shifted the economics of China into an export-oriented model, but also greatly intensified the demand for intercultural communication with the rest of the world. According to Wei and Fei, in the past few decades, with deepening reform, an open-door policy, and increasing demand (particularly as a consequence of China's recent entry to the WTO), English is by far the most widely studied foreign language in China (Wei & Fei, 2003, p. 43). This claim is backed up by many statistics. In 1957, at the height of Russian's popularity in Chinese schools, there were only around 850 secondary school English teachers in the whole country. By 2000, this figure had astonishingly risen to about 500,000 (Bolton, 2002). According to Bolton's statistics, the estimated number of English speakers in China was 200 million, yet according to a newspaper report in the *People's Daily* (2006, March 27), the number of English learners in China has passed the 300 million mark. Among the 300 million English learners, those who are in secondary and tertiary education add up to 100 million. The former teacher and self-made millionaire Li Yang, aptly coined by Newsweek 'the Elvis of English' for his star appeal (McCrum, 2010), has made a business empire out of successfully commercializing China's fixation with learning the English language.

It could be claimed from the above-mentioned statistics that the current high use and status of English in China is going to have important and far-reaching consequences, especially for the languages and cultures of China, and it is of prominent interest to probe into the motivation of English learning. Cole (2007) argues that English in China has usually been viewed as a means to economic gain and has elaborated this argument through Grin's categories of social, private, market and non-market value. According to Bolton (2002), from the 1980s English began to receive increased attention in the national curriculum as well as outside, as evidenced through the popularity of the Test of English as a Foreign Language (TOEFL) and Business English diplomas, the growing number of English media and newspapers in China as well as Chinese students pursuing studies overseas.

> A foreign language is an important tool of interacting with other countries and plays an important role in promoting the development of the national and world economy, science and culture. In order to meet the needs of our Open Door Policy and to accelerate socialist modernization, efforts should be made to enable as many people as possible to acquire command of one or more foreign languages. (1993 English syllabus of China, cited in Adamson & Morris, 1997, p. 21)

In addition to the tangible benefits from learning English, knowledge of English has become a form of 'cultural capital' (Bourdieu, 1984, p. 47) *par excellence* and may easily be regarded as one of the most influential forms of symbolic capital in China. As Hu (2009, p. 49) puts it: 'Access to such knowledge [of English] is intertwined with the availability and deployment of other types of capital, creates relations of power, and leads to both symbolic and material profits.' Access to, and furthermore, the display of English offer opportunities to exhibit the qualities of taste, social status and membership of elite circles of knowledge.

With regard to these relations, in this paper, Chinglish is used as a resource for making sociolinguistic statements. And a sociolinguistic account raises various questions, such as whether a typology of Chinglish is possible; whether attempting such a typology leads to meaningful claims regarding its symbolic value; and how geographical content analysis might be helpful in this exercise. In the next sections of this paper these and other relevant questions are addressed.

Methodology

For this paper, a corpus of 382 pictures from 32 locations was taken into account. All pictures date from the year 2010. In total there were 33 contributors including the two authors. All pictures were provided in digital format to the first author via his website www.chinglish.de. Contributors came from 15 different countries, including China, the US, Germany and a dozen others. The picture content was put into an Excel-sheet and categorized. The following categories were deemed relevant: Photographer, location, content, languages used and in what order, date (year/month). The content was further categorized into: 'Propaganda Chinglish' which is usually issued by government offices (such as 'be friendly and harmonious' at Hangzhou's West Lake), 'Over-literal Translation', which translates Chinese into English word by word ('step forward near civilization' in a restroom in Shanghai), 'Grammatical Mistakes', ('Bed no smoking' in a hotel room) 'Gibberish Chinglish', ('Free yourself from the misery of a existence' over a DVD shop in Shanghai, Pudong, which features something completely different in Chinese), 'Social Register Mistake' ('No chaotic doodle' in Kaohsiung, Taiwan), 'Typo Chinglish' ('Construting' instead of 'Constructing'), 'Irrelevant Wording', whose content does not make sense in its context ('Bathroom' instead of 'Mind your head'), 'Pinyin', appearance of Pinyin where unnecessary or simply no English ('Time files so fast Chao Fan' on a watch on sale in central Beijing), 'No mistakes', which are Standard English signs ('No naked fire' at Yulongxueshan in Yunnan), 'Commercial/ Direction/Information sign' (e.g. signs that feature a 'Notice to tourists') and 'Issuing authority' that probes into the speakers on the signs (such as the Public Security Bureau or private spa resorts in Hainan).

In the naming of the categories and further reference in this paper, the umbrella term of 'mistake' is simply used to cover all linguistic divergence from Standard English without partiality in the estimation or endorsement of any received version of Standard English. The two categories of 'Over-literal Translation' and 'Grammatical Mistakes' are foreseeably going to have some overlap, yet it is clear from the Chinglish data corpus that these two categories are distinct from each other, in that a sign that features over-literal translation is not necessarily faulty in grammar and vice versa. For example, in the West Lake area in Hangzhou city, there is a sign which states 'Orioles singing in the willows' with an arrow pointing to the willow woods on the lake bank. This is a case of literal translation of the Chinese version of this spot which is quite picturesque. '柳岸闻莺' describes willow woods that extends along the lake bank with birds chirping. This translation, although reflecting a strong Chinese aesthetic taste and diction, is grammatically correct. Other examples such as 'In Hopes that will Bring to Me' on a wedding planner's brochure is grammatically confusing yet not a translation of the Chinese text. Thus these two categories are first considered separately with acceptance of possible overlaps.

It is worth noticing that in the statistical analysis of the Chinglish data, it happens that one Chinglish example may feature in more than one category. This is to say that a Chinglish sign could be 'Over-literal Translation' and 'Grammatical Mistakes' at the same time, for example 'Smoked Umbilical' as a sign for a medicinal massage shop in Shanghai's Gubei District. Thus the statistical analysis is based on mistake counts instead of actual Chinglish example numbers, which means that the total number of 573 does not refer to the number of Chinglish examples used in this study, but refers to the total number of mistakes. The error percentages are – unless otherwise stated – all calculated in relation to this absolute figure.

Thirteen pictures had to be taken out of the corpus, either due to technical reasons (too dark, too fuzzy) or because the content was a double entry. One picture did not fall into the category of Chinglish, but was in fact a Lisu language[6] sign transcribed in Latin letters in Gongshan County in Yunnan. The remaining 369 pictures were treated as the corpus for this study. The analysis of this corpus entails statistical, geographical and content analysis.

Results

Introduction of the results

As shown in Table 1 the category with the highest number of language mistakes (182) is 'Over-literal Translations', closely followed by 'Grammatical Mistakes' (178). In third place and already substantially smaller is the category 'No mistakes' with 76 hits. 'Propaganda Chinglish' comes in second-last with 8 hits. The category with the least number of errors is 'Social Register Mistake' (4).

Table 1. Typology of Chinglish files.

Mistake category	Absolute number	Percentage of total number of mistakes
1. 'Propaganda Chinglish'	8	1.40%
2. 'Overliteral Translation'	182	31.76%
3. 'Gibberish Chinglish'	25	4.36%
4. 'Social Register Mistake'	4	0.70%
5. 'Typo Chinglish'	45	7.85%
6. 'Grammatical Mistakes'	178	31.06%
7. 'Irrelevant Wording'	38	6.63%
8. 'Pinyin'	17	2.97%
9. 'No mistakes'	76	13.26%
Total	573	100%

Propaganda Chinglish

This category features signs with an official educative message and an official register. Examples are 'Be friendly and harmonious' or 'Law ruled Chengdu, harmonious dreamland'. A mere 1.40% of the corpus falls under this category. In relation to other mistake categories: 37.5% of 'Propaganda Chinglish' featured mistakes from 'Over-literal Translation' and 'Grammatical Mistakes'. There are no 'Social Register Mistakes' or 'Typo Mistakes' to be found in this category.

Over-literal translation

This mistake category showcases translations with a strong connection to the grammar structure of the Chinese original. Examples are 'no climbing avoid injury' or 'Beware of the electricity to leave the radiation' or 'Grass blue under the foot is forgiving'. As shown in Figure 1, 79.12% of the over-literal translation mistakes also feature grammatical mistakes. This is the highest correlation of two categories found in this study. Other existing, but much less relevant, correlations are to be found with 'Typo Chinglish' (6.59%), 'Irrelevant Wording' (4.95%) and 'Pinyin' (2.2%).

Gibberish Chinglish

Here, the English translation or translation into other languages is either unintelligible or no connection exists between the Chinese original and the English translation. Examples are: 'Free yourself from the misery of a existence' for a DVD shop or 'Theretrdspectientower' at a historic building in Shaanxi's provincial capital Xi'an. The figure for Gibberish Chinglish is low with 4.36%.

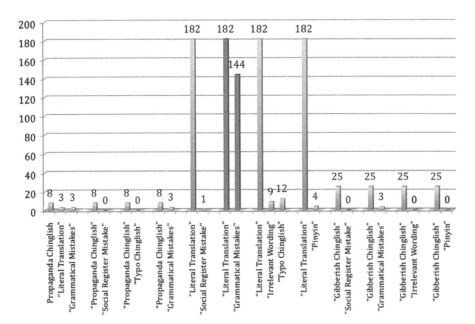

Figure 1.   Relativity between Chinglish mistake categories.

Social register mistake

The social register used in this type of sign is unconventional or even outright offensive to the reader of the English translation. Examples are: 'No chaotic doodle' on a sign in Kaohsiung, Taiwan or the 'Senyo Anus & Intestine Hospital' in Shanghai. It is the lowest category in this study with 0.7% of the total number of mistakes.

Typo Chinglish

This category features signs with minor typographical errors, such as misplaced letters or a missing word?. Examples are: 'Be crreful of the steps' or 'Implant Clinic, Department of Esthetic Dentistry', both from Luzhou (Sichuan), or 'Rescouse saving starts from little things' in a hotel in Shanghai. 7.85% of the total number of mistakes belong to this category.

Irrelevant wording

Signs with irrelevant wording feature translations that exist as a correct statement but bear no relation to the Chinese original. Examples are: 'help the red cross needy' where needy is not in the Chinese original or 'extracorporeal shock wave lipolysis' where the Chinese original does not feature the word 'extracorporeal'. 6.63% of the total number of mistakes belongs to 'Irrelevant Wording'. 31.58% of these mistakes also feature grammatical mistakes.

Pinyin

In this category signs feature only partial English translations with elements of the Latin transcription system for Chinese characters. Examples are: 'Dangxin pengtou' (Mind your head, Shanghai), 'Fresh Jingcai' (Freshly cleaned and diced vegetables) and 'Luo Shi & Style' (Luo Family medical cosmetics, both Luzhou). 2.97% of the mistakes belong to this category.

No mistakes

In this category signs feature no mistakes and are error-free. It should be noted however that this is a purely grammatical category. In terms of content the result can still be regarded as highly unconventional. Examples are: 'Medical times' (Beijing) which besides its name is a 100% Chinese language popular science medical journal available at kiosks and in supermarkets. Or: 'I love therefore I am' claims the slogan of a manga-style comic spokesperson for the Hangzhou city government (seen in Shanghai). 13.26% of the total error corpus belongs to 'No mistakes'.

Commercial/information/direction signs

A basic differentiation was made between signs with a commercial purpose and signs that provide non-commercial information to the reader, including warnings, guidance or instructions (see Figure 2). Examples are: 'Xing Long Fire Equipment Centre' in Chengdu, 'No Naked Fire' in the Jade Dragon Snow Mountain Scenic

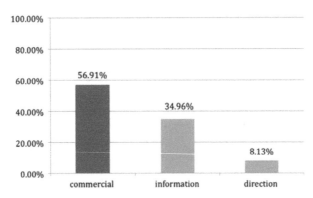

Figure 2. Overview of purpose categories.

Area in Yunnan or 'Please do not spit everywhere' (Yibin, Sichuan) or 'Get a right direction at the exit'. The absolute majority of signs (56.91%) are commercial, one third (34.96%) are information signs and 8.13% are direction signs.

Issuing authority

In this category the focus is on whether the sign provides information about the issuing bureau for the sign or another responsible authority. Examples are: '北京达文海·物业管理有限公司保安部, Beijing Darwin Haikai Property Management Co. Ltd. Security Office' (where *Dawen* 达文 as a translation for Darwin is unconventional in itself) or '广州市客运交通管理处, Guangzhou Passenger Transportation Administration Bureau'. Here, only the information and direction signs of the previous category '*Commercial/information/direction signs*' were taken into account to establish whether or not the communication between the public and the respective institutions or authorities takes place anonymously. Or is there information on the respective bodies available on the sign to react to? Tellingly, only 20.13% of the signs carry information on the issuing authority.

Tourism signs

Signs were categorized as tourism signs when one of the following two aspects were present: Either the signs were situated in an officially declared tourist site, such as the Tiger Leaping Gorge in Yunnan or the Giant Buddha in Sichuan. Or signs were found in sites that were not officially proclaimed tourist spots but might attract or feature tourists, such as public parks or hotels, nature reserves, Metro systems and airports. Under a fourth (23.58%) of the Chinglish corpus is thus classified as tourism signs. Of these Hangzhou features the most signs (26.44%) followed by Shanghai (25.29%), and Beijing (9.20%).

Location and concentration

If we take a more detailed look at where the 369 Chinglish findings come from (see Figure 3), we find that Hangzhou takes the lead with 18.70%, with Beijing coming in second at 16.26%, and Shanghai taking third place with 15.72%. Luzhou is fourth at 14.91%, Yibin fifth with 10.03%, and the remaining 28 locations including

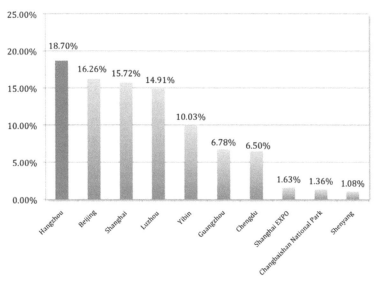

Figure 3. Ranking of locations with Chinglish findings.

Guangzhou (6.78%) and Chengdu (6.50%) in the single-digit realm. The remaining 23 locations were all below 1% and have been removed for reasons of clarity.

Language combination

Figure 4 shows that 82.93% of the analyzed signs feature Chinese-English translations in this order. 10.57% feature English only and 2.71% display English in combination with Pinyin. The remaining nine categories all stay below 1%.

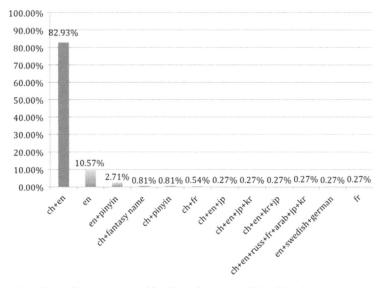

Figure 4. Ranking of language combinations found on Chinglish signs.

Discussion

The number of Propaganda Chinglish signs is very low, given the commercial nature of more than 90% of the corpus, and represents a striking difference from what Pinkham (1998) noted in her research on official newspaper articles. It is additionally striking that more than a third of officially produced signs that aim at instructing or educating local residents feature grammatical mistakes and over-literal translation. Given the official nature of these signs the 'mistake' rate is rather high. Either the production process is carried out unprofessionally or Chinese messages such as 'Develop lawed Chengdu together, share the law fruit together' were translated in the vernacular, and in a way of thinking and expressing that is difficult to translate into the English language for machines and humans alike. The sign is actually trying to say: Let us develop a Chengdu ruled by law and let us enjoy the results of this endeavor.

The greatest concentration of mistake categories is in over-literal translation. Furthermore, in more than 79% of the cases signs with over-literal translations also display grammatical mistakes. One may speculate about the reasons behind this. Two options seem the most probable: option one suggests that the language skills of the sign translators or producers are low and the vernacular used is different than what is needed to produce a non-literal and semantically correct translation. To substantiate this option, further research is needed that deals specifically with the sign production process itself. The second option hints at the highly probable situation that a great deal of the featured translation is not actually done by humans, but by translation software.

A short excursion into the issue of machine translation

It is likely that many sign manufacturers (and 'press-ganged' translators such as the recently matriculated university graduate in charge of public relations who is suddenly given responsibility for the production of bilingual company signs) are actually relying on free online software such as iciba.com or fanyi.cn.yahoo.com to generate the characteristic word-by-word translations. The general problem here is, as Hutchins (2008) notes, that

> much of the language used on the Internet is colloquial, incoherent, 'ungrammatical', full of acronyms and abbreviations, allusions, puns, jokes, etc. – this is particularly true for electronic mail and the language of chatrooms and mobile telephones. These types of language use differ greatly from the language of scientific and technical texts for which MT [Machine Translation] systems have been developed.

Since this is not necessarily the case with official signs, another problem nevertheless might have a considerable impact on machine-based translations. As Hutchins (2008) puts it:

> The Internet has also encouraged somewhat less scrupulous companies to offer online versions of electronic dictionaries (or phrase books) as 'translation systems'. Anyone using such products for translating full sentences (and text) is bound to get unsatisfactory results – although if users do not know anything of the target languages they will be unaware of the extent of the incomprehensibility of the results.

To further substantiate the last point we selected eight of the existing Chinglish collection's more prominent phrases and ran translation quests on five popular websites that offer free online translation services.[7] As can be seen below, the outcome[8] is not only pure Chinglish, but sometimes quite similar to what has been found on the corresponding public signs.

Example 1

Original Chinese: 先下后上文明乘车
Original English: After first under on, do riding with civility

(1) After first under on, the civilization rides in a carriage
(2) Go down upper, civilized riding of queen first
(3) After descending first up, the civilization goes by car
(4) After the jump, civilized ride
(5) Under on, the civilization rides in a carriage after first

Example 2

Original Chinese: 小草有情你当有意
Original English: Love the litter grass

(1) The grass feels emotion you when intends
(2) Small grass has feeling you should have a mind to
(3) The small grass has feeling you to be to have intention to
(4) When you intend to large and enthusiastic
(5) The grass feels emotion you when intends

Example 3

Original Chinese: 注意安全请勿戏水
Original English: Noticing security Don't play water

(1) Pays attention safely please do not play with water
(2) Pay attention to safety not play with water please
(3) Noticing the safety pleases not drama water
(4) Do not playing in the water safety
(5) Pays attention safely please do not play with water

Example 4

Original Chinese: 文明参观讲究卫生
Original English: Visit in civilization, Pay attention to hygiene

(1) Civilized visit Is fastidious the health
(2) Civilization is paid a visit to Pay attention to hygiene
(3) Civilization visit Pay attention to hygiene
(4) Civilization tour Stress health
(5) The civilization visits Is fastidious hygienic

Example 5

Original Chinese: 残疾人厕所
Original English: Deformed men toilet

(1) Disabled person restroom
(2) Deformed man toilet
(3) Disable and sick person's toilet
(4) Disabled toilet
(5) Disabled person restroom

This, of course, can hardly be called translation, but is much closer to decoration. Whether or not a translation is purely meant for ornamentation and not for information needs further substantiation. The results certainly do not speak in favor of someone who cares much about the adequacy of a translation. Tellingly, it is the Translator's Association of China (TAC) itself that shows dissatisfaction over the state of mind of some of its customers:

> The sad thing for translators is that when people discover wrong translations, they invariably pinpoint their fingers at the individual translators who have done the particular translation job, not aware that the root cause lies with the ignorance of the need for professionalism on the part, first and foremost, of administers or those who have failed to give out translation jobs to the professional translator. (Huang & Huang, 2009)

The presented examples in this short excursion do not aspire to be representative. The point is made, though, that further research into the issue of translation software and how its usage has an impact on the translation quality has to play a considerable role.

The number of Gibberish signs is low. The most important insight with regard to this category is the relationship with sign types. Ninety-two percent of Gibberish signs are commercial. This fuels the assumption that in the commercial realm the focus is more on decoration than on information but not to the point of complete unintelligibility. Regarding 'Social Register Mistakes' numbers are even lower. Fewer than 1% of the mistakes fall into this category. Findings from the collection on www.chinglish.de such as 'This toilet is free of washing – Please leave off after pissing or shitting' (from Liaoning capital Shenyang in 2007) hint at that the actual figure might be higher.

Typographical type errors are surprisingly low, at fewer than 8%. This suggests a higher production quality than assumed. The translated syntax is mostly correctly stenciled or printed on the respective billboard, sign or any other carrier of text, the problem of the sign lies much more in the quality of the translation itself with more than a third of the mistakes resulting from over-literal translation and/or grammatical mistakes.

With 31.06% grammatical mistakes is the second-highest ranked error category. It may be explained by low English competency or the well-known inability of translation software to fully grasp the syntax and grammar structure of a sentence. Many signs such as 'Develop lawed Chengdu together, share the law fruit together' (Chengdu) or 'Hurry go? Don't! Rush to walk again' (Shanghai) clearly illustrate the problem of over-literal translation in close combination with grammatical mistakes.

Equally low with Typo Chinglish are mistakes from the category 'Irrelevant Wording'. 'Appropriate Parking' instead of 'Reserved Parking Space' or 'Flush Fire Hydrant' where no 'Flush' exists in the Chinese original. Fewer than 3% of the total number of errors are related to the appearance of Pinyin. Examples such as 'Fresh Jingcai' or 'Spicy Sansi' or 'Guangzhou QunYe Glass Organism Factory' fuel the speculation that most of the Pinyin errors result from machine translation with the translation software unable to recognize and correctly transfer the used wording.

About an eighth of the mistake corpus is error-free. This number is high regarding the motivation of the respective contributors to send in a picture reporting a sign with supposedly broken or incorrect English. 'Be patriotic and obey the law' which also belongs to Propaganda Chinglish is actually error-free but for an English native speaker the sign features a rarely heard schoolmasterly tone. Here an actor-centered perspective would likely prove helpful in trying to work out the differences in reception between different audiences. A Chinese citizen might react quite differently to a sign that communicates an educative message such as the above-mentioned than a non-Chinese.

It is not surprising to find one of China's major tourist hotspots, Hangzhou, taking the lead in this study, not only in terms of total number of errors, but also in the category of tourism signs (more than a fourth of the tourism signs). The city is not only a major attraction to foreign visitors, but also one of the highest-ranking domestic tourism locations in China. The area around the West Lake, Hangzhou's main attraction, is fully equipped with Chinglish signs, such as 'Refectory' for 'Restaurant' or 'The pleasant-boat pier of no.1 lakeside park'. Contrary to what might be expected, only around a fourth (23.58%) of the Chinglish corpus actually consists of tourism signs. The vast majority do not. Based on this study, it is safe to say that the main reason for Chinglish is not the tourism industry, but commerce, and especially retail, outside it. With the highly commercial nature of the corpus it is reasonable to speculate that English words are placed on billboards, road signs and product labels not only for the purpose of giving information but also for the purpose of appearing cosmopolitan and attracting domestic consumers as well. And it is here that we find ornamental English has value as symbolic capital in the Bourdieusian sense. It displays a certain level of sophistication, an international identity, even if the displayed English is faulty or features non-standard English wording. According to Bourdieu the connection between economic and cultural capital is established through the mediation of the time needed for acquisition. And '... the system separates the holders of inherited cultural capital from those who lack it' (Bourdieu, 1998, p. 20). Chinglish, on the other hand, is the result of a display of supposed cultural capital, the supposed knowledge of English, an attempt to leapfrog into a circle of high cultural capital.

For further analysis of the data we used GeoTwain[9] to visualize the localization of the Chinglish findings used for this paper's corpus analysis. The tool provides georeferencing data for each Chinglish sign but also produces a timeline to show where and when the sign was spotted. With a larger corpus the software might be able to establish a clearer picture of the geographical spread of Chinglish and dynamic changes over time: for example, whether incidences of Chinglish increase in times of higher international exposure, such as the Beijing Olympics 2008, or not. The results of this study nevertheless suffice to demonstrate that Chinglish is a nationwide phenomenon not limited to the rich coastal areas in the east of the country.

Suggestion for further studies

The present study deals with Chinglish findings from 2010 only and therefore has its limits in terms of corpus size and time span. Further studies are needed to include a larger corpus with a longer time span. Additionally, further research has to include the actual sign production process and a more anthropologically informed analysis of the data to find out what is the motivation to produce bilingual signs at all. Qualitative interviews with shop owners and customers need to establish whether customers are aware of a shop's bilingual signage and in what way the bilingual signage may or may not shape a shop's brand and image. Secondly, more research needs to be done regarding signs issued by official institutions. Here the main focus must be on the system of proofreading and control of translations. Additionally, the lack of any institutional name on the majority of official signs suggests a particular style of communication, which needs further scrutiny.

Conclusion

369 Chinglish findings from 2010 were analyzed in this study. 573 errors were found among them. The categories have proven helpful for establishing a preliminary typology of Chinglish but fall short of providing an all-encompassing picture. Suggestions for further research include a longer time span that can help to shed light on changes in error-production over several years.

The cause of Chinglish on signs is the translator through the typology analysis of the Chinglish corpus. In a striking difference from what Pinkham noted in her research on official newspaper articles, propaganda Chinglish occupies less than 10% of the corpus of bilingual signs. Furthermore, more than one third of Propaganda Chinglish features grammatical mistakes and over-literal translation. Thus, an in-depth study might provide highly interesting insights into the actual sign-production process from interviewing decision makers and translators.

Regarding the type of signs, it is noticeable that the majority of signs are of a commercial nature and more than 80% of the signs carrying non-commercial information or guidance or warnings do not feature the institution, official bureaus or authorities that issued the signs. Here further research is needed to elaborate further on the rather decorative use of English in the commercial realm, where the existence of non-Chinese lettering is used to establish an appearance of cosmopolitanism or the status of an international brand. The anonymous nature of the communication between the issuing institution and the public is another striking feature of the present research results. Is the sign itself too unimportant to leave an identifying body or is feedback on the sign even undesirable and the authority responsible not wanting to be bothered? With one fourth of the corpus dedicated to tourism, it is a major contributor to Chinglish signs, but is not the biggest. Tourism is not the main cause for Chinglish, it is the commercial environment around it. Signs with rather instructive messages, such as 'be patriotic and obey the law', have another function, to show foreign visitors that the local government is educating its citizens and, secondly, to let the local population know that the foreigners know about it too. This double-layered communication structure is highly intriguing and needs further in-depth field research. It has to go beyond the need to deliver pragmatic, correction-oriented statements on how to improve the nation's public bilingual signage standards, statements that are off-stage again once international events such as the Olympics or the 2010 World EXPO in Shanghai have ended. Chinglish is the result of a nationwide attempt of the official, the commercial and the private realm to bounce China into becoming a twenty-first-century bilingual society. The imperfection of this attempt does not put in question the very endeavor. On the contrary, with the current English craze and an ongoing low-level English language competence, Chinglish will continue to flourish as long as the Chinese travel, and English will remain a linguistic symbol of sophistication and positive public branding in the years to come.

Notes

1. Sometimes trilingual with Japanese or Korean.
2. Public means that no entrance or other kind of fee has to be paid in order to see the signage.
3. Chinglish research is not to be confused with research on China-English, i.e. correct English with endemic terms such as 'Three Representatives' or 'The Gang of Four', research that has grown into an extensive corpus of academic publications since the term was coined in 1980 by Professor Ge Chuangui (Ge, 1980).
4. The database search query did not display any hits for 2010. While the possibility exists that not even one single thesis was produced this year, it seems more likely, though, that data of 2010 has not been entered into the database yet.
5. The perseverance of this English fever is insofar puzzling, as being an English major can, according to the '2010 Annual Report on the Employment of Chinese College Graduates', no longer be regarded as the stepping-stone to a fast track career in the PRC. For the last three years, the maximum number of jobless graduates majored in English, computer science and law (Chinese Academy of Social Sciences, 2010).
6. Lisuyu is a tonal Tibeto-Burman language spoken in Yunnan (southwestern China). It is the language of the Lisu minority as well as lingua franca of other minorities in the region.
7. Used online services (1) http://fanyi.cn.yahoo.com/, (2) http://trans.godict.com/, (3) http://www.iciba.com/, (4) http://translate.google.com/, (5) http://www.onlinetranslation.cn/
8. Garbled translation output is the case with most other languages run through a translation software at the moment, although efforts by Google's ambitious translation project 'Google Translate', which is based on statistical machine translation, are promising; see 'Inside Google Translate' (Google, 2010).
9. Freely accessible at URL: http://kjc-fs2.kjc.uni-heidelberg.de/GeoTwain/.

References

Adamson, B., & Morris, P. (1997). The English curriculum in the People's Republic of China. *Comparative Education Review, 41*(1), 3–26.

Anonymous. (2005, May 26). Welcome the 2008 Games with correct bilingual signs. *China Education and Research Network*. Retrieved December 15, 2010, from http://www.edu.cn/Newswin_1547/20060323/t20060323_127180.shtml.

Bolton, K. (2002). Chinese Englishes: From Canton jargon to global English. *World Englishes, 21*(2), 99–181.

Bourdieu, P. (1984). *Distinction – A social critique of the judgement of taste*. London: Routledge.

Bourdieu, P. (1998). *Practical reason: on the theory of action*. Cambridge: Polity Press.

Chinese Academy of Social Sciences. (2010). *2010 nian Zhongguo daxuesheng jiuye baogao* 2010 年中国大学生就业报告 [Annual Report on Chinese College Graduates' Employment). Beijing: Shehui kexue wenxian chubanshe.

Chinese University Alumni Association (CUAA). (2010). *2010 Zhonguo daxue pingjia yanjiu baogao* 2010 中国大学评价研究报告 [2010 evaluation of the Chinese Universities Ranking]. Retrieved December 15, 2010, from http://www.cuaa.net/cur/2010/.

Cole, S. (2007). The functionalist account of English in China: A sociolinguistic history. Retrieved September 23, 2010, from http://homes.chass.utoronto.ca/~cpercy/courses/eng6365-cole.htm.

Facebook group 'Save Chinglish – China's disappearing culture'. (2010). Retrieved October 12, 2010, from http://www.facebook.com/group.php?gid=4441472314.

Flickr photo group 'Chinglish'. (2010). Retrieved October 11, 2010, from http://www.flickr.com/groups/chinglish.

Ge, C. (1980). Random thoughts on some problems in Chinese-English translations. *Chinese Translator's Journal*, *1*(2), 1–8.

GeoTwain (2010). Retrieved December 23, 2010, from http://kjc-fs2.kjc.uni-heidelberg.de/GeoTwain/.

Google (2010). 'Inside Google Translate'. Retrieved December 23, 2010, from http://translate.google.com/about/intl/en_ALL/.

Hu, G. (2009). The craze for English-medium education in China: Driving forces and looming consequences. *English Today*, *100*(4), 47–54.

Huang, Y., & Huang, C. (2009, October 13). The translation industry in China: Current development and potential for international cooperation. *TAC Online*. Retrieved November 12, 2010, from http://www.tac-online.org.cn/en/tran/2009-10/13/content_3182787.htm.

Hutchins, J.W. (2008). *Machine translation: A concise history*. Retrieved January 17, 2011, from http://www.hutchinsweb.me.uk/CUHK-2006.pdf.

Liu, D. 刘丹, & Teng, Y. 滕育栋. (2006, March 27). 300 Million Chinese Learning English '三亿中国人学英语 *People's Daily*《人民日报》 p. 11.

Lü, H. 吕和发, & Dan, L. 单丽平. (Eds.). (2002). *Han Ying gongshiyu cidian* 汉英公示语词典 [A Chinese-English Dictionary on Signs]. Beijing: Shangwu yinshuguan.

Lü, H. 吕和发, & Wang, Y. 王颖. (Eds.). (2007). *Gongshiyu Han Ying fanyi* 公示语汉英翻译 [Chinese-English Translation of Public Signs]. Beijing: Zhongguo duiwai fanyi chuban gongsi.

McCrum, R. (2010, June 12). Glob-ish – Powered by the Internet and the global media, English has evolved into the world's language. *Newsweek*. Retrieved May 8, 2010, from http://www.newsweek.com/2010/06/12/glob-ish.html.

Oxford English Dictionary Online. (2010). 'Chinglish' entry. Retrieved September 16, 2010, from http://dictionary.oed.com/cgi/entry/00335104?single=1&query_type=word&queryword=chinglish&first=1&max_to_show=10.

Pinkham, J. (1998). *The translator's guide to Chinglish*. Beijing: Foreign Language Teaching and Research Press.

Radtke, O. (2010). More than errors and embarrassment: New approaches to Chinglish. In J. Liu & H. Tao (Eds.), *Chinese under globalization: Emerging trends in language use in China*. Singapore: World Scientific.

Wei, Y., & Fei, J. (2003). Using English in China: From Chinese Pidgin English through Chinglish to Chinese English and China English. *English Today 76*, *19*(4), 42–47.

Zhang, H. (2003). *Chinese Englishes, History, contexts, and texts* (Doctoral dissertation). University of Illinois at Urbana – Champaign. Retrieved January 8, 2010, from http://www.proquest.com.

Index

Note:
Page numbers in **bold** type refer to figures
Page numbers in *italic* type refer to tables
Page numbers followed by 'n' refer to notes

Abercrombie, N.: and Longhurst, B. 12, 13
Acland, C.R. 18
Adamson, B.: and Morris, P. 95
Ahuvia, A. 42, 47; and Carroll, B. 44, 49
All About Mr Hatterr (Desani) 56
Almeria 2, 6–20; Mini Hollywood 14
Amazon 12
L'America a Roma (Pannone) 14
Anant, V. 57, 60
Angel of the North (Gormley) 67
Appadurai, A. 4, 80
Askegaard, S.: and Madsen, T.K. 47
association 47
August, K. 11
authenticity 3, 44, 47
autobiographies 3, 59–61
avatars 2, 32, 34

Baedeker 84, 85
Bakardjieva, M. 7, 10
Bakhtin, M. 15
Baudelaire, C. 71
Baudrillard, J. 43
Bauer, L.: and Trudgill, P. 84
Bauman, Z. 83
Baym, N. 10
behaviour: consumers 47
behavioural code-shifting 32
Beijing Olympic Games (2008) 94, 105, 107
Beijing Speaks Foreign Languages
    Committee 94
Belk, R.W. 41–2
Benjamin, W. 73
Bennett, G. 56
Berlitz 83
Berlitz Pocket Guide Portugal 84
Betts, T. 13
Beverland, M.: and Farrelly, F. 44, 47
Bhabha, H.K. 2, 22, 61
Big Gundown, The (Sollima) 12, 17
bilingual tourism signs: China 4, 91–108
Bird, S.E. 8
Bluemelhuber, C.: and Rojas Gaviria, P. 42

Boehmer, E. 61
Bolton, K. 95
border crossings 1, 2, 4, 6; real 10–18
borders: virtual 2, 7, 8–10, 18
boundaries: blurring 1
Bourdieu, P. 26, 31, 41, 95, 96, 105
Braithewaite, J. 14, 15
brand: consumption 43; international 5, 106;
    love 44, 49
Breathnach, C. 76
British Empire 54
broken middle 68
Brooke, R. 60
Brooker, W.: and Jermyn, D. 11
Broughton, L. 1–2, 6–20
Bruckner, U. 13
Burnett, R.: and Marshall, P.D. 13
Bye Bye Blackbird (Desai) 55, 57, 58–9
Byram, M. 26

capital 95; cultural 96, 105; economic 105;
    knowledge 10; social network 10;
    subcultural 14; symbolic 96, 105
capitalism: global 54
carnival 15
Carroll, B.: and Ahuvia, A. 44, 49
Catalunya (Spain) 2, 21
categories 27; construction 26
C'era una Volta il Western (Marsili) 7, 13, 18
Certeau, M. de 11, 76
Chandler, D. 43
Chaudhuri, N. 55, 59, 60
Chi-square test 46, 51n
China: Beijing Olympic Games (2008) 94,
    105, 107; Beijing Speaks Foreign
    Languages Committee 94; bilingual
    tourism signs 4, 91–108; economic
    development 93; English media 95; English
    speakers 95–6; Hangzhou 105; intercultural
    communication 95; international image 93;
    Reform and Opening-up Policy (1978) 95;
    students 95; symbolic capital 96; World
    EXPO (2010) 107

China Academic Journals 93
China Daily 93, 94
China Education and Research Network 94
Chinglish 4, 91–108; analysis 95;
   Commercial/Direction/Information sign 96,
   97, **98**, 99–100; definition 92, 93; errors 4;
   Gibberish Chinglish 96, *97*, 98, **98**;
   Grammatical Mistakes 96, 97, *97*, 98, **98**,
   102, 104; Irrelevant Wording 96, *97*, 98, **98**,
   99, 105; Issuing Authority 96, *97*, **98**, 100;
   Mistake Categories 97–100, *97*, **98**, 102;
   No Mistakes 96, *97*, **98**, 99; Over-literal
   Translation 96, 97, *97*, 98, **98**, 102; Pinyin
   96, *97*, 98, **98**, 99, 105; Propaganda 96, 97,
   97, 98, **98**, 102, 105, 106; research 93–4, 95,
   107n; Social Register Mistake 96, *97*,
   98, 99, 104; tourism 106; tourism signs 100,
   100, **101**; Typo Chinglish 96, *97*, 98, **98**, 99,
   105; typology 96, *97*, 106
Christianity 76
cinema 64
Cleef, F. 12, 13, 18
Clifford, J. 71, 80
clothes and fashion 49–50
Cole, S. 95
collective intelligence 10
collocations 50
colonialism 56–7, 61, 62
commercial cultures 41
commodities 3; role 40–52
commodity culture 45
commodity as lens 50
communication: channels 30, 32; technology
   22, 24, 35; virtual 2, *see also* intercultural
   communication
communicative approach 62–3
communicative traits: cultural 26
communion 10
community 68; imagined 13, 17, *see also*
   virtual community
competence: intercultural 1
computer editing software 13
Computer-Mediated Communication (CMC)
   22, 24
conflict: identity 42, 47; intercultural 32
Conradson, D.: and McKay, D. 45
consumer societies 45
consumers: behaviour 47; self-identity 44
consumption 41, 44; and identity 41–2;
   international students 46; patterns 45
contamination 43
copyright laws 11
Cordeiro, M.J. 4, 79–90
corporal indexing 43
cosmopolitanism 5, 106
Crang, P.: *et al* 45, 50
Cresswell, T. 80

critical intercultural semiotic awareness 36
critical semiotic awareness 35
Cronin, M. 66, 69, 70, 71, 77, 82
crossings: semioscape 4, *see also* border
   crossings
cult geographies 13–14
cult media fans 11, 16, 17
cultists 12
cultural capital 96, 105
cultural communicative traits 26
cultural ecosystem 69
cultural flows 3, 40
cultural identity 2, 25, 28, 36, 45, 48, 68
cultural immersion 83
cultural knowledge 35
cultural learning 35
cultural markers 42
cultural mediation 81
cultural norms 62
cultural production 7
cultural theory 3
cultural transmission 75
cultural work 73
culture 1, 4, 23, 25, 80; beyond 67–72;
   commercial 41; emergent 23; English 57,
   61; fan 2, 6, 7, 10–18; folk 11; food 47–8;
   high 68; industry 11; Internet 34; and
   language 3, 63, 75; multiple 36; shock 3,
   82; study of 33; travelling 80, 81; wars 68

Dan, L.: and Lü, H. 93
Davies, A.: and Fitchett, J.A. 45
Deleuze, G.: and Guattari, F. 69
Denzin, N.K. 7, 9
Derringdo 11
Desai, A. 55, 57, 58–9
Desani, G.V. 56
desire assemblage 42
dialogues 87
Diehl, W.: and Prins, E. 2, 22, 34
digital natives 22
Django Challenges Sartana (Squitieri) 11
Dooly, M. 1, 2, 21–39; Vallejo, C. and
   Unamuno, V. 26
Dorling Kindersley 83
Dr Quinn, Medicine Woman 8
DVD players 12

e-cultures 36
e-mail interviews 6, 7
Eagleton, T. 66, 67–8
Eastwood, C. 13, 16
economic capital 105
economic liberalization 62
economy: gift 13
ecosystem: cultural 69

education: English in India 53, 54, 55, 56, 59, 62; intercultural 2
Egypt: Internet 22
elections 22
electronic dictionaries 102
Elphinstone, M. 4, 66, 72–3
emergent cultures 23
emotional attachment 47
enclavic spaces 82
England: imagined 3, 53, 54, 62; Indians in 3, 53–65; real 62
English: as international brand 5; Standard 96
English culture 57, 61
English education: India 53, 54, 55, 56, 59, 62
English language 61, 62, 63, 64
English literary images 55
English literature 55, 56, 58, 60, 61
English media: China 95
English poetry 58, 60
English speakers: China 95–6
Englishness 55, 56, 57, 58, 60, 61, 63, 64
enthusiasts 12
Epp, A.: and Price, L. 41
ESL teaching 24
Esser, H. 54
ethnicity: virtual 30
Eustace, M. 14
Eyewitness Travel Guides Portuguese Phrase Book 87

Facebook 2, 22, 35, 94
familiarity 53, 54, 64
fan cultures 2, 6, 10–18; theory 7
fan fiction 11; writers 11–12
fans: cult media 11, 16, 17; Spaghetti Westerns 2, 6–20
Farrelly, F.: and Beverland, M. 44, 47
fashion 49–50
Fei, J.: and Wei, Y. 95
Ferguson, J.: and Gupta, A. 80
fiction 3, 57–9; fan 11
filming locations: Spaghetti Westerns 7, 14–18
Fishman, J.A. 63
Fistful of Dollars, A (Leone) 6, 14
Fistful of Travellers' Cheques, A (Spiers) 16
Fitchett, J.A.: and Davies, A. 45
Flickr 94
folk culture 11
food: brands 48; cultures 47–8
For a few Dollars More (Leone) 16
Friel, B. 4, 66, 71–2, 73, 74

gender 34
geographies: cult 13–14
GeoTwain 105
Ghosh, S.K. 55, 59, 60–1

Gibberish Chinglish 96, *97*, 98, **98**
gift economy 13
global flows 4
globalization 80–1; linguistic aspects 4
Golden Boot Awards 10
González, F.E. 87
Gonzalez, M.: and Phipps, A. 67, 70, 74
Good, the Bad and the Ugly, The (Leone) 15
goods 41; as informants 41–5; perception 42–4, **43**
Google Translate 107n
Gormley, A. 67, 71
Gorter, D.: and Shohamy, E. 4
Graddol, D. 62
Grant, K. 14
Grayson, K.: and Shulman, D. 43
Gregory, C. 15–16
group identities 28
Guattari, F.: and Deleuze, G. 69
guests 81
Guha, R. 56
guidebooks 82–4, 85, 86, *86*, 87, 88; glossaries 87
Gulia, M.: and Wellman, B. 15
Gupta, A.: and Ferguson, J. 80
Guth, S.: and Helm, F. 22, 23, 26, 30, 35

habitus 41, 47
Helm, F.: and Guth, S. 22, 23, 26, 30, 35
Heyward, M. 34
Hills, M. 13–14, 16, 17
Hinnenkamp, V. 30
Hiro, D. 55, 58
Holliday, A. 42; Hyde, M. and Kullmann, J. 33
Hollywood Westerns 8
Hopkins, G.M. 77
hosts 81
Hu, G. 96
Huang, Y.: and Huang, C. 104
Hutchins, J.W. 102
Hyde, M.: Kullmann, J. and Holliday, A. 33
hyper reality 43

identity 23, 25, 34, 40, 41, 54, 56; conflicts 42, 47; construction 22; and consumption 41–2; cultural 2, 25, 28, 36, 45, 48, 68; education 57; group 28; Indians 53; language 55, 57; literary education 55; literary images 58, 59; membership 21, 27, 36; national 23; offline 27; place 45; politics 68, 70; real world 30; shared 32; Westernized 63–4
Illinois 2, 21
images: English literary 55; multimedia 3
imagined community 13, 17
indexical anchoring 43, 44

indexical signs 42–3
India: British rule 3; English education 53, 54, 55, 56, 59, 62
Indian-English literary texts 56
Indians: in England 3, 53–65; identity 53; literary representations 53–65
individual agency: and social structures 26
informants: goods as 41–5
information and communication technologies (ICT) 35
Ingold, T. 66, 68–9, 70, 71, 73, 75, 76
Instant Messaging 35
intellectual passport 53, 62
intelligence: collective 10
intercultural communication 1, 32, 41, 81, 82, 86; China 95; studies 30; virtual space 2
Intercultural Communicative Competence (ICC) 2, 21, 23, 25–6, 30, 33, 34, 36; teaching 31–2
intercultural competence 1
intercultural conflict 32
intercultural education 2
intercultural learning 2
intercultural sensitivity 31
intercultural third space 30–6
intercutural literacy 2
International Association for Languages and Intercultural Communication (IALIC) 1
international brands 5, 106
international students 3; clothes and fashion 49–50; commodities 40–52; consumption 46; food 47–8; literature 49; music 49; technology 48–9; toiletries 49
Internet 8, 64; culture 34; Egypt 22; electronic dictionaries 102; language 102; media 23; message boards 9, 10
interviews: e-mail 6, 7; semi-structured 46
Isenberg, R. 13

Jack, G.: and Phipps, A. 86
Jasmine revolution 22
Jaworski, A.: and Thurlow, C. 87
Jenkins, H. 10, 11
Jermyn, D.: and Brooker, W. 11
Jordan, T. 9

Keesing, R.M. 66, 68
Kessoux, A.: and Roux, E. 44
kinship 76
knowledge: capital 10; cultural 35
Koch Media 13
Kollock, P.: and Smith, M.A. 8
Kullmann, J.: Holliday, A. and Hyde, M. 33

Lamaj, A. 12
land 3, 4, 66, 72–4, 77
Landon, R.: and St. Louis, R. 85

landscapes 3, 4
language 3, 23, 35, 54, 73; autonomy 87; commodification 81, 88; and culture 3, 63, 75; definition 69; keywords 87; learners 22; local 85–6, 88; mobile 1, 80–1; myths 84; policies 81; pronunciation 83–4; role 1, 81; shared 54; toy versions 87
Language and Intercultural Communication 1
language learning 2, 3, 26, 35; industry 82–3; telecollaborative 22, 23, 33–4
language perception: Portuguese 84–5
language-in-use approach 27
languagers 67
languages to go 84
languagescapes 4, 81
languaging 3, 66–78
learner diversity 34
learning: cultural 35; intercultural 2; language 2, 3, 26, 34, 35, 82–3; telecollaborative language 22, 23, 33–4
Leeds Metropolitan University: Centre for Tourism and Cultural Change 1
leisure travel 1
Leone, S. 6, 8, 14, 16
Leroux, J.: Yoo, S-H. and Matsumoto, D. 32
Levy, P. 10
linguistic landscape 4
linguistic reassurance 85
liquidity 83
literacy: intercutural 2
literary images: English 55
literary representations: Indians 53–65
literary texts 60, 61; Indian-English 56
literature 3, 49
Living Language 84
London, S. 81
Lonely Planet Phrase/Guide Books 83–4, 85; *Portuguese Phrase Book* 85, 86, 87, 88
Longhurst, B.: and Abercrombie, N. 12, 13
Lü, H.: and Dan, L. 93; and Wang, Y. 93
Lury, C. 80

Mache, E. 12
machine translation 102–6
McInnes, A. 17
McKay, D.: and Conradson, D. 45
Madsen, T.K.: and Askegaard, S. 47
Magnificent Seven, The (Sturges) 14
Making of Per un Pugno di Sogni, The (Kiral) 15, 16
Marshall, P.D.: and Burnett, R. 13
Marsili, M. 7, 13, 14, 15, 17, 18
Marx, K. 3
Massey, D. 18
Matalo (Canevari) 13
material goods 2–3; and self 41; transnational experience 40–52

Matsumoto, D.: Leroux, J. and Yoo, S-H. 32
media 23; cult 11, 16, 17; English in China 95; pull 8; social 22
mediation: cultural 81
membership 23; identities 21, 27, 36
Menon, K.P. 59
message boards 9, 10
migration: common language 54; forced 1; human 80; international 54
mimicking native 61
mind 69
Mini Hollywood (Almeria) 14
misunderstandings 30, 32
mobile language 1, 80–1
mobility (mobilities) 1, 79; frictionless 81
modernity 42; Western 56
moment identification 34
Monceri, F. 40
Montagnon, D. 85, 86
Moodle 2, 21, 37n
Mooij, M. de 47–8
Morgan, N.: and Pritchard, A. 88
Morricone, E. 17
Morris, P.: and Adamson, B. 95
multilingualism 79, 81
multimedia images 3
music 49
My English Journey (Ghosh) 55, 59, 60–1

naming phenomenon 72
national identity 23
nationalism 56
Net-zines 13
network exchanges 21
network-based language practice 22
new communication semiotics 2
norms: cultural 62
nostalgia 44, 48
Nudge, J. 8, 15, 18

offline identities 27
Omar, M.: and Penman, C. 1, 2–3, 40–52
Omoniyi, T. 34
on-line fandom groups 10
Once Upon a Time in the Autumn (Isenberg) 13
Once Upon a Time in the West (Leone) 14
O'Regan, J.: Wilkinson, J. and Robinson, M. 1–5
O'Reilly, T. 22
Ozden, C.: and Schiff, M. 54

Pannone, G. 14
Parthasarthy, R. 60
participant observation 6, 7
Passage to England, A (Chaudhuri) 55, 59, 60
passport: intellectual 53, 62

Pearce, P.L. 82
Penman, C.: and Omar, M. 1, 2–3, 40–52
People's Daily 95
Per un Pugno di Sogni (Marsili) 15, 17
perception 68–9
petty producer 13
Phipps, A. 3–4, 66–78, 83; and Gonzalez, M. 67, 70, 74; and Jack, G. 86
phrase books 4, 82–6, *86*, 87, 88; *Lonely Planet Portuguese Phrase Book* 85, 86, 87, 88
Pied Beauty (Hopkins) 77
Pinkham, J. 92–3, 102
poaching 11, 12
podcasts 2, 25, **29**, 37n
Poelzl, V. 85, 86
poetry: English 58, 60
polyglossia 79, 81
Portmeirion Hotel Village 15
Portugal: *Berlitz Pocket Guide* 84
Portugués para viajar 85
Portuguese: Brazilian 84; European 84; *Lonely Planet Portuguese Phrase Book* 85, 86, 87, 88; phrase books 4; to go 84, 87; tourist guides 79–90
Poster, M. 30
Prensky, M. 22
Price, L.: and Epp, A. 41
Prins, E.: and Diehl, W. 2, 22, 34
Prisoner, The 15, 16
Pritchard, A.: and Morgan, N. 88
pronunciation 83–4
propaganda 91
pseudo-Americana 14
pull media 8

quantitative surveys 45

racism 58, 59
Radtke, O. 94; and Yuan, X. 4–5, 91–108
Raja, R. 57
Random House 84
reading: meaning-making 11
Reading as Poaching (de Certeau) 11
reality: hyper 43
rebellion 11
relational thinking 69
Revolving Man (Anant) 57
Rheingold, H. 7, 8, 9, 10
Robinson, M.: O'Regan, J. and Wilkinson, J. 1–5
Rodriguez, L. 9
Rojas Gaviria, P.: and Bluemelhuber, C. 42
Rose, G. 68, 70–1
Run, Man, Run (Sollima) 16–17

St Louis, R.: and Landon, R. 85

scapes 4, 80
Schembri, S. *et al* 43–4
Schiff, M.: and Ozden, C. 54
Schivelbusch, W. 88
sculpture 71
Second Life 2, 21, **29**, 31, 32, **32**, **33**, 35, **35**, 37n; scavenger hunt 24, **24**
Seiter, E. 7
self: core 42; extended 42; and material goods 41
semi-structured interviews 46
semio-texts 4
semiotic awareness: critical 35, 36
semiotics: new communication 2
sensitivity: intercultural 31
Serpent and the Rope, The (Raja) 57
shared identity 32
shared language 64
Sharma, M. 3, 53–65
Shohamy, E.: and Gorter, D. 4
Shulman, D.: and Grayson, K. 43
signs: indexical 42–3; translation 93
Six of One 15, 16
skills continuum 12
Skype 2, 21, 37n
Smith, M. 9–10
Smith, M.A.: and Kollock, P. 8
social action 26
social media: elections 22
social network capital 10
social structures: and individual agency 26
societies: consumer 45
Sollima, S. 16
spaces: transitory 18
Spaghetti Western Web Board 2, 7–18
Spaghetti Westerns: DVDs 12–13; fans 2, 6–20; filming locations 7, 14–18
Sparrow's Flight, A (Elphinstone) 4, 66, 72–3, 75–6
spatiality 18
speckled scape 76–7
Star Trek 18; fan fiction writers 11–12
stereoptyping 62
Stewart, S. 87
student teachers 2, 21–39
students: Chinese 95, *see also* international students
subcultural capital 14
subjectivity 56
surveys: quantitative 45
symbolic capital 96, 105

tactics 76
taskscape 66, 76–7
teacher-talk 27

teachers: culture 27; education 21–39; identity 27, 28; student 2, 21–39; virtual community 30
teaching: ESL 24; ICC 31–2; practices 25; sequences 2; units 24
technology 48–9; communication 22; new 6, 11, 12, 18
telecollaboration 2.0 projects 23
telecollaborative exchange 26–7
telecollaborative language learning 22, 23, 33–4
television 64
Test of English as a Foreign Language (TOEFL) 95
texts 4
thinking: relational 69
third space 2, 21–2, 25, 34; intercultural 30–6
Thurlow, C.: and Jaworski, A. 87
toiletries 49
tourism 1, 6, 54, 79, 81, 88, 89, 91; communitas 15; industry 82; international 82, 88; mass 14; miniaturizing technique 87; new 14; western related 15
tourism signs: bilingual (China) 4, 91–108
tourist encounters 82–4
tourist guides 1, 4, 79–90, *see also* guide books; phrase books
traditioning 75
translation 3–4, 4, 66–78, 106; machine 102–6; relational mode 76; role 70; as sensory activity 69, 71, 72; signs 93
Translations (Friel) 4, 66, 72, 74–5
translators 69, 71
Translator's Association of China (TAC) 104
transnational experience 2; commodity culture 45; material goods 40–52
transnational objects 3
transnational virtual community 6
travel 1; leisure 1; virtual 1
travellers 80
travelling cultures 80, 81
Trevelyan, C. 55
Triangular View, A (Hiro) 55, 58
Trudgill, P.: and Bauer, L. 84
Tuco Tours 14
twitter 22

Unamuno, V.: Dooly, M. and Vallejo, C. 26
Universitat Autònoma de Barcelona (UAB) 23, 25, 28, 32
University of Illinois Urbana Champaign (UIUC) 23, 24, 28, 29, 32, 33
University Research Ethics Committee 45
Urry, J. 1, 14, 15

Vallejo, C.: Unamuno, V. and Dooly, M. 26
Van Cleef, L. 13, 16, 17

video cameras: digital 13
virtual borders 2, 7, 8–10, 18
virtual communication: evolution 2
virtual community 2, 7, 8–10, 18, 22, 23, 25, 27; definition 9; teachers 30; transnational 6
virtual community of practice (VCoP) 28
Virtual Community, The (Rheingold) 8
virtual ethnicity 30
Virtual Learning Environment (VLE) 37n
virtual togetherness 2, 10
virtual travel 1
Viswanathan, G. 55–6
vodcasts 25, 37n
Voicethread 2, 21, 24, 27, 37n

Wallach, E. 16
Walt, V. 22
Wang, Y.: and Lü, H. 93
Warkschauer, M. 62–3
wars: culture 68
Web 2.0 tools 22, 25, 34
Wei, Y.: and Fei, J. 95
Wellman, B.: and Gulia, M. 15
Western All'Italiana 13, 14

Westerns: Hollywood 8, *see also* Spaghetti Westerns
Wild East 12
Wilkinson, J.: Robinson, M. and O'Regan, J. 1–5
Williams, R. 75
Wiseman, R.L. 25
World Bank 54, 68
World EXPO (2010) 107
World Trade Organization (WTO) 95

X Files 8, 14, 18

Yoo, S-H.: Matsumotot, D. and Leroux, J. 32
Yuan, X.: and Radtke, O. 4–5, 91–108

Zhang, H. 92
Zoho **31**

www.routledge.com/9780415857956

Related titles from Routledge

Mobilities and Forced Migration

Edited by Nick Gill, Javier Caletrío and Victoria Mason

This book sets out the ways in which theories of mobilities can enrich forced migration studies as well as some of the insights into mobilities that forced migration research offers.

The book covers the challenges faced by both forced migrants and receiving authorities. It applies these challenges to regions such as the Middle East, South Asia and East Africa. In particular, the chapter on Iraq to Jordan foced migration tests the sincerity of the concept of Pan-Arabism; the chapters on Bangladesh and Ethiopia deal with the more historically familiar variables of warfare and famine as drivers of forced migration.

This book was published as a special issue of *Mobilities*.

Nick Gill is senior lecturer in human geography, Exeter University, UK.

Javier Caletrío is a researcher based at the Centre for Mobilities Research at Lancaster University, UK.

Victoria Mason is lecturer in the School of Politics and International Relations at the Australian National University.

Jul 2013: 246 x 174: 168pp
Hb: 978-0-415-85795-6
£85 / $145

For more information and to order a copy visit
www.routledge.com/9780415857956

Available from all good bookshops

ROUTLEDGE

Related titles from Routledge

Migration and Citizenship Attribution

Politics and Policies in Western Europe

Edited by Maartin Peter Vink

How do states in Western Europe deal with the challenges of migration for citizenship? The legal relationship between a person and a state is becoming increasingly blurred in our mobile, transnational world. This volume deals with the membership dimension of citizenship, specifically the formal rules that states use to attribute citizenship.

Migration and Citizenship Attribution observes various trends in citizenship policies since the early 1980s, analysing historical patterns and recent changes across Western Europe as well as examining specific developments in individual countries.

This book was originally published as a special issue of the *Journal of Ethnic and Migration Studies.*

Maarten Peter Vink is Associate Professor of Political Science at Maastricht University, The Netherlands.

June 2012: 246 x 174mm: 160pp
Hb: 978-0-415-50283-2
£85 / $145

For Product Safety Concerns and Information please contact our EU
representative GPSR@taylorandfrancis.com Taylor & Francis Verlag GmbH,
Kaufingerstraße 24, 80331 München, Germany

Batch number: 08165860

Printed by Printforce, the Netherlands